I0211959

Panic Early, Panic Often

Other books by Pam Johnson-Bennett and Kae Allen

Cookies for Dinner (White River Press)

Other books by Pam Johnson-Bennett

Think Like a Cat (Penguin Books)

Cat vs. Cat (Penguin Books)

Starting from Scratch (Penguin Books)

Psycho Kitty (Ten Speed Press)

Panic Early, Panic Often

more true stories from two moms in their quest to survive motherhood

Pam Johnson-Bennett and Kae Allen

White River Press
Amherst, Massachusetts

Panic Early, Panic Often

First published 2016 by
White River Press
P.O. Box 3561
Amherst, Mass. 01004
www.whiteriverpess.com

Book design by
Douglas Lufkin, Lufkin Graphic Designs
www.LufkinGraphics.com

Illustrations and cover by
Norris Hall
www.norrishall.com

ISBN: 978-1-887043-18-2

Library of Congress Cataloging-in-Publication Data

Johnson-Bennett, Pam, 1954-
Panic early, panic often : more true stories from two moms in their quest to survive motherhood / Pam Johnson-Bennett and Kae Allen.
pages cm
ISBN 978-1-887043-18-2 (pbk. : alk. paper)
1. Johnson-Bennett, Pam, 1954- 2. Allen, Kae, 1963- 3. Motherhood. 4. Parenting. 5. Mothers--United States. I. Allen, Kae, 1963- II. Title.
HQ759 .J67
306.874'3--dc23

2015016623

Dedicated to Scott, Gracie, and Jack, the loves of my life.

Dedicated to David, Matt, Christi, and Jess,
you are my heart and soul.

Acknowledgments

The Two Loons would like to thank Linda Roghaar for your support, talent, and dedication to writers. Thank you to Norris Hall for your amazing illustrations and the ability to capture us as we really are.

From Kae: I would like to thank my husband, David. Your love makes me want to strive every day to be a better person. I would like to thank my kids, Matt, Christi, and Jess for letting me tell the world how much I adore them. Finally, I would like to thank Pam for pushing me to come on this adventure. Without all of your support, I would still just be an accountant regaling my clients with stories of my wonderful, wacky family.

From Pam: Thank you to my husband, Scott. Your belief in me all these years is something I truly cherish, and I hope I have lived up to all that you see in me. Thank you to my children for making it so much fun to be your mom. Every day with you is a precious gift. Thank you to my co-author, Kae, for your friendship, talent, patience, and incredible sense of humor.

Contents

About the Two Loons

Catching up with the Two Loons

When you last left Pam and Kae, you were learning about how they survived the first five years of motherhood. Believe it or not, they did survive, and their kids still haven't required long-term therapy due to their mothers' parenting skills—but there's still time. If you're thinking the two moms got the hang of motherhood at that point and became the June Cleavers of the neighborhood you'd be wrong . . . very, very wrong.

If this is your first time delving into Pam and Kae's tales from the motherhood trenches, we need to get you up-to-speed. Pam and Kae are two friends who couldn't be more opposite when it comes to their mothering styles. This difference, along with their innate survival instincts to laugh (insert bizarre hyena laugh here for proper effect), their way through the world of dirty diapers, separation anxiety, misbehaving husbands, and the bumpy ride on the "potty train," brought them together to share their confessions about what goes on behind the doors of two homes that appear quite normal and sane to the outside world.

Cookies for Dinner came about because Pam and Kae felt mothers didn't need another "how to" book on parenting. What mothers needed was to know they're not the only ones who stand on the checkout line sharing potting training horror stories with anyone who will listen.

In Cookies for Dinner, Pam and Kae bravely told about how one unexpectedly learns the poop capacity of a car seat, what it feels like to have your toddler lock you out of the house while wearing less-than flattering swimwear, and how to remove a crow from the nursery while changing your child's diaper. Then there's the fact that when nursing, your breasts are treated like a fast food take-out window or that a ravenous infant can create more suction than industrial-grade vacuum cleaners. Let's not forget how a sausage, egg, and cheese biscuit can cause a pregnant woman to do strange things, the circumstances under which it's acceptable to hose your child down in the front lawn, why it's ok to vacuum immediately before a tornado, and just how much a minivan can hold before it explodes.

Pam and Kae know what mothers need . . . they need to laugh and realize they're not alone on the roller coaster ride of motherhood.

In case you're wondering how these two moms could still have even more confessions to tell, rest assured, in Pam and Kae's lives there are countless embarrassing moments yet to be told.

Cast of Characters

The Bennett Family . . .

Pam: Pam is the germ-eradicating half of the Two Loons. She became a mother late in life, at the age of 47 through adoption. Her family lovingly accepts her OCD and in fact, it has provided great comic material for them at family gatherings. They have also made peace with their mother's rather unique career—being a cat behavior expert and star of the Animal Planet UK show Psycho Kitty. Pam has so far managed to worry, obsess, and laugh through 13 years of motherhood, though the fact that many people assume she's Gracie and Jack's grandmother still causes her to cringe a bit.

Scott: Pam's husband of more than 17 years. Scott is a dedicated, loving, and very messy guy. Ok, let's just call it like it is—Scott is a big kid who doesn't see anything wrong with leaving his dirty clothes three-point-five inches from the hamper. Being a father has truly enabled Scott to experience a second childhood. Pam has accepted the fact that Scott will always be referred to as the "fun" parent, except in the eyes of Griffin, the family dog. Griffin still eyes Scott with suspicion and is probably hoping his stay is only temporary.

Gracie: Pam's daughter. Adopted at four months old, Gracie has been a take-charge, strong-willed girl from day one. She is also extremely tender, kind-hearted, spiritual, and adventurous. As a baby, Gracie could unbutton, unzip, and remove any article of clothing or diaper known to man in a split second. Duct tape became the only way to keep a diaper on the child. As a toddler, she managed to lock her mom out of the house, perfectly time her glass-shattering screams to ensure maximum ear damage, talk to anybody and everybody in public restrooms. She also referred to her father as Bob for almost two months. Gracie takes her role as older sister very seriously and frequently reminds her little brother that her 21-month head start over him in life has given her tremendous maturity and wisdom.

Jack: Pam's son and Gracie's younger brother. Jack was also adopted when he was four months old. You have to look closely if you want to spot Jack in the house because he's always in motion. That blur you see going by is probably him. He is a motorized child with the metabolism of a hummingbird. Anything in Pam's home that is scratched, dented, taped, or just completely broken can be credited to the lightning bolt that is Jack. Pam is fairly sure Jack's first words were, "Oops, sorry." Jack depends on his older sister to guide him through the childhood jungle, open his juice bottles and come up with believable excuses for why Jell-O is dripping from the ceiling or why there's a dried-up slug in his underwear drawer. Jack is sensitive, extremely smart, and very musically gifted. His dream is to become a professional guitarist.

The Allen Family . . .

Kae: Kae is the fearless Mommy-leader of the Allen crew. Whether eradicating a giant black crow from the house with a butterfly net or banishing the monsters that go bump in the night, Kae was the go-to Mommy in the Allen house when the panic set in. During this period of time Kae spent her days trying to juggle the needs of her growing family and her growing accounting practice while still trying to find time to throw a few bowling balls each week.

David: David is Kae's wonderful, sensitive, fun and exasperating husband of over 30 years. David's sensitive nature when it came to the children made him a much better maternal figure than Kae. He spent countless hours playing games with the kids, riding bikes, and reading stories. He was one of the few husbands in our generation that dealt willingly with the yucky parts of parenting. He changed toxic diapers and cleaned up more than his fair share of bodily fluids the children deposited on the carpets and sofas. David's only downside during this phase of the Allen children's lives was his inability to handle discipline. In the years that have passed, Kae has begun to think he was suffering from a form of "children's" Stockholm syndrome. He spent so much of his time playing with the kids that he began to sympathize with their plight of having such a strict Mom. But no matter what few negatives there are to Kae's wonderful husband, there are ten times as many positives. Kae believes that between the two of them, they made one stellar parent.

Matt: Matt, aka Matthew, is the oldest of the Allen children. Being the first-born male meant that Matt took the lead in most of the early Allen children adventures. Matt was the first to lead in a game of pirate ship on the sofa on a stormy afternoon or lead the bicycle parade around the backyard. It was very clear in the Allen children hierarchy: Matt was the leader and the girls were his ever-faithful minions.

Christi: Christi, aka Christina, aka Steenie, is the middle child in the Allen brood. She was Matthew's sidekick, and played her role as the gentle half of the "Allen Girls" with enthusiasm. If you wanted to see where Christi was, all you had to do was jingle your car keys and she came running. Christi was David's faithful companion on many a Home Depot run, and she was Kae's loyal companion. She may have been released from the womb, but that didn't mean she didn't find every opportunity to snuggle right back next to her Mom.

Jess: Jessica, aka Jess, aka Peepers, is the baby of the Allen brood, but don't you dare tell her that. From the time Jess could talk, she was the first to let you know that she wasn't a baby. Jess was Kae's little firecracker. If her brother and sister could do it, then so could she, never mind the six-year age difference. If Matt could ride a bike, so could she. If Christina could do a backbend, so could she. From the time Jess could walk, she was joined to

Christi's hip. Jess was so intent on being just like her sister that the two morphed from being referred to as individuals to simply being called the "Allen Girls."

Panic Early, Panic Often

Chapter 1

Who Would Have Thought?

Waiting for a Gate

By Kae

Nursing in public was a touchy issue for me. I didn't mind whipping out a breast in the privacy of my own home. Heck, half the time I was walking around the house attending to the thousands of other household duties while a child sat comfortably in the crook of one arm munching away. But my philosophy about breast-feeding in public is simple: Just because you attach a child to it doesn't mean it isn't still a breast.

Breasts are the oft-hungered-after touch trophies of adolescent males. They are the first sign of maturity in a young woman. They have a place in our history and society of a sensual nature. Latching a kid onto one of them does not change what they are and how the people around you view them. A breast is not a bottle or a pacifier. It's a breast. To me, it's similar to my husband trying to convince me that because boxers have legs they aren't underpants. They're still your underpants, and you shouldn't be standing in the front yard surveying storm damage in them.

I did my best to keep my nursing private. If we were visiting relatives, I would sequester myself in another room until my breast could be placed back into the proper attire for public viewing. Generally, if we were going somewhere that would require a feeding, I brought a bottle of mother's milk. This way, Christina could eat and I could maintain what little dignity a mother of two can muster.

The other problem with nursing Christina in public was that as soon as she started eating, she would begin kicking her feet and moaning loudly in delight. This was not something she did with a bottle, just the breast. So we nursed in private—most of the time.

Two months after Christina was born, I found myself boarding an airplane with my new baby daughter and my two-and-a-half-year-old son. We were going to spend two weeks with my mother. David, always the bright one, had decided that he could not take the time off from work. So he planned to fly down for a couple of days at the end of the trip and then fly home with us. Since he was a lawyer just starting out, it didn't seem implausible that he couldn't get the time off.

When I was making the plane reservations over the phone (this was back in the dark ages when you actually had a cord on the wall phone in the kitchen, and you stood there while arranging flights with the ticket agent of the airline you wanted to fly on), I informed the ticket agent that I would be flying with my newborn baby and my two-and-a-half-year-old son. A sympathetic clucking came over the phone. "And you have two adults?" the ticket agent asked.

"No, just me, my son, and my daughter."

More sympathetic clucking. "I will put you in two seats, first row past the bulkhead. That way you'll have room for your son to play on the floor and not disturb the other passengers." It was a brilliant idea. This was when the airlines insisted that you check your child's car seat with your other luggage. It didn't really bother me that Matthew would not be in his car seat. Unless I attached a parachute to it, I didn't think it would be much protection if the plane went down.

In preparation for our flight, I carefully planned the packing of the diaper bag. Matthew and the potty train had not yet arrived at their destination. Having a newborn and a semi-potty-trained little boy on a plane seemed like enough stress for one day. Figuring out how to get the three of us into the cramped little airplane bathroom seemed a little over the top. So into the diaper bag went 12 newborn diapers, six stage-three diapers, two full changes of clothes for each of the children, one large box of pre-moistened baby wipes, one large bath towel to wrap Christina in when she took her bottle (so if she vomited I could keep it encapsulated), one kitchen garbage bag to put the bath towel in, plastic bags for "dirty" disposals, nursing pads and a clean bra for me along with a top that wouldn't look too wrinkled if it had to come out of the overstuffed diaper bag in an emergency, two bottles of mother's milk for Christina, one Ziploc bag of Cheerios, and a bright red box of animal crackers for Matthew. Matthew also packed his little blue train case that his great-grandmother Allen had given him to keep his toys in. He stuffed it full of all the toys he thought he would need for his long trip.

When we got to the gate to board our plane, the voice from the overhead speaker called for all passengers with small children or those who needed boarding assistance to come to the front. We kissed Daddy goodbye. I slung the weighted-down diaper bag over my right shoulder and propped the infant car carrier with Christina in it on my left hip. Matthew carried his little blue train case and held my hand to "make sure I didn't lose the tickets" that I was clutching. Several wheelchair-bound passengers and a couple of families made it to the line before we did and were rapidly being shuttled toward the gangway to the plane. Matthew was being wonderful for a two-and-a-half-year-old having to stand in line. Before we got up to the ticket agent, the overhead speaker announced the boarding of the next set of passengers. A large line of people formed behind us.

Matthew handed the ticket agent our tickets and was rewarded with a pair of little golden wings that were safety-pinned to his collar. The agent leaned down to Matthew and said, "Okay, little man, you take your mommy and sister right down that hallway."

Matthew nodded his affirmative and we headed happily for the gangway.

About ten feet past the threshold Matthew came to a screeching halt. He was having none of this walking down a tube thing. In retrospect, I can understand his distress. The gangway had begun to bounce slightly with the weight of the people walking through. To adults this is just a minor sensation; to a two-and-a-half-year-old it was terrifying. Without missing a step, I raised Matthew up by his arm and rested his diaper-clad bottom on my right hip. And down the gangway we went, a woman of about five-foot-three, 100 pounds soaking wet, car seat resting on her jutted-out left hip, diaper bag hanging heavily from her right shoulder, and a two-year-old with his arms around her neck in a death grip holding onto a little blue train case that had come to rest at the back of her head, his bottom trying to keep purchase on the non-jutting-out hip.

At the door of the plane I asked Matthew if he wanted to get down now, but he just buried his head into my neck and tightened his grip. The flight attendant wanted to take the diaper bag for me, but it was stuck underneath Matthew, and Matthew wasn't budging. She attempted to take the little blue train case from Matthew's hand, but he wasn't letting some strange woman take his toys. I side-stepped down the narrow aisle, being careful not to bop anyone on the head. Finally, we made it to our seats.

I was arranging our things on the floor in front of me when I began to notice other passengers getting on the plane. I was astounded that several of the men openly glared at me. A couple of women came past us and began whispering loudly enough that I could hear them say they didn't want to sit anywhere near us. At the time I was mildly offended. These perfect strangers had judged my children as disruptive without even knowing them. (Twenty years later, I was boarding a plane to Las Vegas with my husband. David led the way to seats in front of a harried looking woman with a two-year-old child in the seat next to her. I guided David several rows back. Now I understood why the older women didn't want to sit by my kids. They had done their time and didn't want to share in mine.)

The plane was on schedule and everything was going fine. Matthew sat in the seat next to me and we watched as the plane lifted off the ground. He was mesmerized by the buildings and cars down below and was perfectly entertained until the clouds obscured his view. Of course, we had discussed his behavior on this flight while we'd been getting ready to go: He would be in public; he knew how to behave in public. "Other people on the plane won't want to be stuck up there with a little kid screaming his head off," I had told him. "If you don't behave yourself, you will get a spanking right in front of all the people you're disturbing." I had looked him straight in the eye so he knew there was no wiggle room. If I said I was going to do something, it was guaranteed to happen.

"If you're really good during the flight, when we're getting ready to land you can have this piece of gum," I'd added, handing Matthew the stick of gum to put into his pocket. Matthew almost never got to have gum, so this was a great bribe for good behavior. It also would help his ears pop when the airplane began to descend. I thought I had covered all the bases. I had made a list and checked it twice. I had thought of everything that could go wrong and had come up with a preemptive strike to thwart even the slightest possibility of a threat.

The flight was wonderful. Matthew and I colored while Christina slept. When I fed Christina her bottle, Matthew had cookies from the flight attendant and a cup of juice. Christina took the whole bottle, burped like a little lady, and went right back to sleep. When she woke again after half an hour or so, I changed her diaper. Then it became apparent from her rooting around that she was hungry again. The last thing I wanted was for her to start crying the "I'm hungry" cry that was the signal for my milk to let down. This four-hour flight was stretching my limits as it was; I didn't need any help. I fed Christina the last of the bottles and she drifted off to sleep again.

All was well until we began our descent. Matthew had the gum in his mouth and was chomping happily away, watching the cars and buildings come closer and closer. Christina began to fuss. I tried to get her interested in a pacifier and then her thumb, but she wasn't to be fooled. She wanted to nurse and she wanted to do it now. I tried to distract her with bouncing and cooing but she was having none of it. She knew I was the holder of the goods, and she wanted them turned over at once.

As I'd exhausted all my other options and Christina's cries began to intensify, I pulled the large towel out of the diaper bag and covered my upper body with it. I slid Christina underneath the towel and began nursing her just before we touched the ground. The pilot came on the intercom and announced that due to some airport congestion we did not have a gate yet, but we would be assigned one as soon as possible. The plane taxied a little ways and then came to a stop. The pilot shut off the engines and the passenger compartment fell silent—except for the loud moans of a delighted little girl getting her lunch.

Trouble in the Jungle

By Pam

My son, Jack, absolutely loves his stuffed animal collection and used to arrange them all in bed with him every night. His cheetah, giraffe, elephant, lion, white tiger, and monkey all had assigned sleeping positions. Jack insisted that they all get the pillow while he curled up at the bottom of the bed. After several nights of arguing with him about this and having him cry when I displaced his animals, I gave up and let him place his little jungle friends wherever he wanted. After he fell asleep, I sneaked in and placed his stuffed buddies at the foot of the bed, and transferred him to the pillow position. He never suspected that I was the one behind this maneuver. I can only assume he thought the animals had migrated in the wee hours of the morning.

His massive collection of stuffed animals is now kept in his closet in various bins and boxes: I'm certain that it far exceeds the stuffed animal capacity law for the closet. When doing laundry, I take my life into my hands if I try to hang his shirts up. Animals have exploded out of the bins like fuzz-covered missiles. Many have also caused my vacuum cleaner to overheat when it unexpectedly sucked up a monkey by the arm or a zebra by the tail. I have never told Jack the reason why his baboon's left arm is significantly longer than its right arm. Being wound around the brushes on the vacuum does wonders for limb enhancement.

Jack loves watching any television show about animals (so long as none of them get eaten by other animals). Any time he can catch a glimpse of animals, he's thrilled. If it's a choice between cartoons or lions on the savannah, the lions win every time. We are also regulars at our local zoo. If there's a day off from school and weather conditions aren't bad, we can be found making the rounds, and of course, we can't leave there without stopping at the gift shop for yet another over-priced stuffed animal.

In keeping with Jack's love of all things animal- and jungle-related, his room has a jungle theme. There are huge, floor-to-ceiling pictures of animals on his walls, and jungle animals line a high shelf that goes around his room.

When Jack was about five, I thought it would be a wonderful adventure for the four of us to have dinner at the Rainforest Café, a jungle-themed restaurant that had recently opened in our town. Many parents of my kids' friends had told me about it and how much their children absolutely loved the place. They even had kids' nights. I thought this would be the coolest adventure for my little Jungle Jack. The big night was six days away.

I started preparing the kids right away. We marked the day on the calendar so we could count down to Saturday. I told them how exciting the place was, that they had animals (not real ones), and how it would be just like walking through a jungle. Jack could hardly contain himself. I told the kids that they had to be on their best behavior until Saturday. I think Jack and Gracie surprised even themselves with how well behaved they were all week.

Finally Saturday came. We headed to the mall where the restaurant was located. We put our names on the waiting list and were told there was an hour-long wait. No problem, we said, because in the front of the restaurant was their rainforest retail store. I knew we'd end up having to buy some little overpriced item for the kids, but for the time being, they were thrilled just to look at and touch everything.

We all put puppets on our hands and acted out a little impromptu performance; Jack tried on a gorilla mask; Gracie squealed at the rubber frogs and lizards. She spotted more girlie-type things at one point and I headed there with her, while Scott stayed with Jungle Jack as he looked at the gross reptile stuff. Gracie picked out a rainforest pencil, and I bought it for her, then we met up with Jack and Scott. I saw that Jack was holding a small stuffed giraffe. Our retail purchases seemed to be taken care of for the night, and I was relieved that we apparently got away with not having to explain to the kids that we weren't going to buy the life-size gorilla, no matter how much they whined.

After waiting a little over an hour, our name was called and we were instructed to get in a line of people waiting to be seated. The kids were hungry and very anxious. I kept telling them that it would all be worth it.

"I'm gonna' see an elephant," Jack said to everyone on line behind him. "I'm gonna' see an elephant and lots of animals."

The hungry people standing behind us just politely smiled. They had their own impatient kids to deal with.

Jack tugged on my sleeve. "Mommy, can I touch the elephant?"

"I don't know dear, probably not. But you'll get to see him," I said. "Oooh, it's going to be so much fun."

We finally reached the front of the line and as the restaurant hostess was about to ask us how many in our party, Jack blurted out, "Where's the elephant?"

"You want to see the elephant?" she asked him with a big smile. He nodded. "Well, it just so happens I have a table right next to the elephants just for you." Jack jumped up and down. The long wait really was worth it.

Suddenly, as we were walking to our table, the room got noisier. The jungle sounds were very loud: The farther into the restaurant we ventured, the louder they got. As we sat down at our table, we saw that we were literally right next to three huge elephants.

"Did that elephant just move?" Scott asked the server as he came to take our drink order.

"Yes," he answered, "but that's nothing. In a few minutes they'll start making noise like the beginning of a stampede."

Jack may have liked all things jungle, but that included my being able to control the volume on the TV. An elephant stampede five feet away from us was another story. I was getting worried that this dining adventure was about to get too intense.

"How loud does it get?" I asked the server, trying to be heard over the increasing noise of the jungle birds.

"Very loud. And do you see those monkeys over there?" He pointed to our left. "They'll start screeching. They also do a rainforest thunderstorm every fifteen minutes where there's loud thunder and flashes of lightning."

My children were deathly afraid of thunderstorms. I had been working so hard on helping them feel more comfortable in storms, and now their mother was about to throw them right into the middle of a tropical storm from which there was no escape.

"Scott, I think we should leave," I said across the table, trying to maintain my Calm Mommy voice. Scott nodded, but before we could get up the lightning flashed and there was a loud crack of thunder. Then the elephants started their trumpeting, the monkeys responded with their screeching opera, and the lion issued a loud roar. I was about to put my arms around Jack when I noticed the two seats next to me were empty. My kids were no longer sitting at the table; they were curled up underneath.

I got down under the table with them. "Babies, it's okay. This is all make-believe. We're going to leave though."

Jack was crying and Gracie, who appeared to be in shock, was just seconds away from crying. I lifted my wailing, trembling son out from under the table, and Scott took Gracie in his arms. As we started walking to the door, Gracie swung her legs around Scott's waist in an attempt to get as close to him as possible. Unfortunately, her Dora the Explorer sneaker hit the just-filled glass of iced tea belonging to a fellow diner. Down the cold tea spilled into the lap of the neatly dressed woman. This innocent bystander was understandably upset, but Jack's arms around my neck were starting to cut off the oxygen supply to my brain. I needed to act fast. I dug into my purse, tossed enough money on the table to cover their entire dinner and dry cleaning bill, and said I was sorry. A long apology was certainly called for, but I had to get my kids out of the restaurant before the next simulated thunderstorm or stampede. We then carried our children out of the restaurant, past the retail area, and back out into the normalcy of the mall. We just kept walking until we couldn't see or hear a trace of the Rainforest Café.

We finally reached a quiet area of the mall and sat down on a bench to regroup. Both kids were starting to calm down. I took them to the restroom so I could wash their faces. We then distracted them by talking about getting hamburgers and French fries, followed by a little ice cream.

At this point, we were getting close to Jack and Gracie's bedtime. We ducked into one of the hamburger places in the mall and let them order whatever non-nutritional, fried, salty, fatty things they wanted, followed by whatever sickeningly sweet ice cream sundae concoction they named. Guilt ruled.

As we ate dinner, Scott and I stared at each other in shock. We didn't want to talk about what happened because we were both terrified to even mention the words "rainforest" or "elephant."

How terrified of thunderstorms were my kids going to be now? Would I have to tear down the huge elephant mural on Jack's bedroom wall?

By the time dinner was over, both kids were leaning against us, half asleep. We carried them to the mall exit that was the farthest away from the Rainforest Café. Our car was on the other side of the parking lot, so Scott went to retrieve it while I sat on a bench with two exhausted children.

As we placed Jack and Gracie in their car seats, I glanced up at the sky to make sure there were no clouds. The cherry on top of this disaster would've been encountering a real storm on the drive home.

As we were driving home, Scott asked me how much I paid for the giraffe Jack was holding.

"I didn't buy that," I said, "didn't you?"

"I didn't buy it. I thought you did."

We looked at each other. Nobody had paid for it. I put my hand over my mouth.

I looked back at my two sleeping, recently traumatized kids. "I'm not going back there to return it," I said. On my next shopping trip to the mall I could go to the cashier at the Rainforest Café and pay for the giraffe. The Bennetts have our faults but we're not giraffe thieves.

Scott and I decided that we'd overlook this crime, due to the traumatic events of the evening. We vowed never again to utter the words Rainforest Café in front of our children until they were of college age.

Fortunately, the Rainforest incident didn't affect Jack's love for all things jungle, although both kids did plead with me to never take them there again. And, for many months after, whenever Scott and I mentioned going out to dinner, one or both kids would shriek, "No, not the Rainforest Café!"

Apparently, Jack has no memory of where his cute little giraffe came from. And I have no intention of telling him.

Just in case you're wondering, the giraffe has since been officially purchased.

No Fair

By Kae

All new parents bring to the table of parenthood a host of idealistic thoughts on child rearing. We vow never to utter the words "Because I said so!" in answer to our child's incessant questioning of our parental proclamations. We read every All the Goofy Advice About Babydom book we can get our hands on in an effort to be the best parent possible. Based on our countless hours of research, we vow never to curse in front of the children, never to discipline a child when we are angry, and for my husband, David, never to allow candy or cookies to pass their lips.

According to conventional wisdom, ingestion of sugar by a child results in the dreaded "sugar rush." This is the phenomenon that occurs just after a parent hands a child a sugar-laden treat with the pronouncement, "I know you will be wild as a buck as soon as you eat this candy bar, but here you go anyway." Sure enough, no sooner has a child ingested a cookie then he/she is vibrating with nervous energy, thrashing about wildly, ignoring every word of correction that comes out of his/her parent's mouth.

Abolishing the evil of sugar in the Allen household was an admirable goal, although it was short-lived. By the time Matthew was two, he had been introduced to cookies by his great-grandmother, who made the sweet little treats with Matthew in mind. Matthew was the recipient of tiny sugary tidbits from Great-Grandma any time David wasn't looking. I was also an accomplice in Matthew's dabbling in the realm of sugar. When he began potty training, he became well acquainted with the fruity little morsels known as Skittles that took up residence in small bowls behind every toilet in our house. And—after Christina was born—on very rare occasions of excellent behavior in the grocery store, I rewarded Matthew with one of the small candy bars wrapped in brightly colored cellophane found on the bottom shelf at the checkout line.

As an interesting sidebar, none of my children ever experienced a sugar rush. In our household, you were expected to act appropriately no matter what the circumstances. There were no "Get out of jail free cards" because you had ingested a sugar-laden treat or because your bedtime was 20 minutes ago. I expected my children to behave themselves. Period, no excuses.

By the age of three, Matthew had hit the growth charts in the 95th percentile for height and the fifth percentile for weight. "Growth spurt" was his middle name. This physical diversity created years of shopping trauma for both mother and child. When purchasing pants for Matthew, there was an ongoing war between his ankles and his belly button. If the pants fit him properly in the waist, the legs came halfway up his calves, giving him the look of a child always on guard for the next flood. If the legs were long enough, the waist was so large that if he sneezed the pants would fall down to his ankles.

Summer was my favorite time. The warm weather meant that we could spend countless hours playing in the yard and taking long walks around the neighborhood. Warm weather also meant Matthew could be dressed in shorts and short-sleeved shirts. Finally, we could buy pants that fit in the waist and not worry about the length. Shirts could be purchased to fit across his shoulders without concern about the three-quarter-length sleeves.

Sadly, all good things must come to an end. One of the first cool afternoons in September found me carrying Christina in her car seat on my jutted-out left hip with a fully packed diaper bag slung over my right shoulder, holding Matthew's hand and dragging him, whining, toward the little boy's section of the local Marshalls.

"Why do I have to get new pants?" Matthew whined in an effort to thwart the mission at hand.

"It's getting cold outside and none of your long pants fit you anymore. We have to get you some new ones."

"I just like these ones," Matthew said as he looked down at his raggedy end-of-summer shorts.

"You can't wear short pants in the winter time, Matthew. Your little legs will freeze off. Do you want blue knees?" I quickly began pulling different styles of blue jeans in Matthew's size off the shelves and piling them on top of Christina in her car seat. Christina had a full tummy and was happily waving her hands and kicking her feet under the growing piles of clothes loaded onto her.

"Look at these, Matthew, they have cool little pockets on the sides where you could put your toy cars. When we try them on in the dressing room you can put one of your cars in to see if it will fit, okay?"

"I don't want to," Matthew whined.

I quickly snagged a couple of long-sleeve sweatshirts with colorful pictures of Batman and Spider-Man on them. We made a beeline for the nearest dressing room and piled in. I put Christina down on the floor in the corner, pulled the mound of clothes from on top of her, and tossed them in the middle of the floor.

"Okay, up with your hands, little buckaroo," I said as I made a pretend gun with one hand and tickled Matthew out of his shirt. "Down to the Scoobys, mister," I said as we pulled his pants off. Matthew noticed that there was a big mirror in the dressing room and we took turns making funny faces and Matthew showed off his "muscles," posing in the mirror like his favorite action figures.

I sat on the floor next to a pile of denim in the dressing room and helped Matthew into the pair of jeans with the little car pocket on the side. Digging around in the diaper bag, I found one of Matthew's cars. He quit whining about how the legs were scratchy and became engrossed in the job of trying to get the car down into the little pocket.

Suddenly, I became aware of the feeling that all women my age associate with an early arrival of "their special friend." One more item left out of All the Goofy Advice About Babydom books in my reference collection was the section on menstruation and the nursing mom. No one told me that the term "tidal wave" would be the best description for the beginning of each period I had while nursing my girls. Nor was there any reference to the fact that while nursing, the menstrual cycle would have a top secret, need-to-know-basis time schedule of its own. Needless to say, the surf was up, and I was on the beach without a surfboard. I had to find a bathroom immediately or Matthew would not be the only one shopping for new pants and Scooby-Doo underwear this lovely fall day.

In a small panic, I quickly pulled Matthew's shirt on over his head, hefted the diaper bag onto my right shoulder, pulled Christina's car seat up to my left hip, grabbed Matthew's hand, and took off into the store in search of the nearest ladies restroom.

One of my flaws as an individual is that when I am in a crowded area, I lose all ability to navigate. I can't stand to go to Walmart because all those yellow smiling faces distract me to the point where I can't remember what I went in for. In malls, I always become disoriented, inevitably resulting in several moments of confusion over where I parked my car. So here I am, a woman with a serious "friend" issue, laden down with a baby in a car seat and an over-stuffed diaper bag, dragging a whining little boy through the store, attempting to read the signs above each section that appear to be written in hieroglyphics.

Finally I stumbled upon a sales clerk. Breathlessly, I told her that I had an emergency need to find the ladies room. Sympathetically, she looked down at Matthew with his shirt slightly askew and assumed that my little man was in need of the potty. Instead of giving us directions, the clerk said, "Follow me," and within a hairsbreadth we were safely in the ladies room.

I bolted to the last stall in the bathroom, dropped the diaper bag to the ground, and slid Christina's car seat into the stall. It is at this point that a parental dilemma presented itself. Here I was, the woman who was petrified that her child would be abducted. I was also the woman whose three-year-old would think she has been eviscerated by the toilet monsters if he caught just a peek of the carnage going on in his mom's Scooby-Doos. I had just gotten Matthew fully on board the potty train. I didn't even want to imagine what would happen if he got it in his head that there were monsters in the potty.

Time was of the essence; the decision had to be made: Leave Matthew outside the stall door and tempt the fate of the abduction god or have Matthew somehow squeeze into the narrow stall with me and Christina and take my chances that I could explain to a three-year-old the normal reproductive cycle of the average human female.

In the end, I decided that the chances of Matthew being abducted were about as miniscule as the chances that he would understand the menstrual cycle, so I decided to let him stand outside the door.

"Matthew, mommy has to do girl things in the potty. I want you to stand right here in front of the door so I can see your feet the whole time, okay?" I said to him as I quickly entered the stall, stepped over Christina, turned, and closed the door.

"What girl things?" he asked as I watched his blue tennis shoes shuffle impatiently outside the stall door.

"Just things that mommies have to do sometimes," I said, stripping out of my ruined underwear and throwing them into the metal sanitary napkin container. "When I get done, we'll go back and finish picking out your jeans." I rummaged around in the diaper bag searching desperately for the stash of tampons I never left home without.

"What you doing in there?"

"Do you like the sweatshirt with Batman or Spider-Man best?" I asked as my hand finally found the cellophane-covered savior.

"Batman is scratchy. I want Spider-Man."

"Okay, we can get the one with Spider-Man on it," I said in an effort to continue to occupy Matthew while I attended to my own business.

My heart leapt to my throat when I heard the door to the bathroom open. The small space erupted into conversation as several women came in at the same time. "Matthew, stay right there. Mommy will be finished in just a second," I said as I rushed to finish the project at hand, sure that my child's feet would disappear from under the stall door at any second. In my haste, I noisily ripped the cellophane wrapper from the tampon.

"Hey, no fair. You're eating a candy bar," Matthew indignantly bellowed from the other side of the stall door. I could hear the gale of giggles from the women who had just entered.

The Fun One

By Pam

I learned a lot about my spouse after we had children. The husband who so bravely killed the big spiders and left work at the busiest time to change my flat tire in the shopping mall parking lot is someone, I soon realized, who shrinks in terror at the sight of baby poop. The man who wakes up from a sound sleep if he hears so much as a twig snap outside could now sleep through the high-pitched wailing coming through the baby monitor that sat right on the nightstand. The man who owns a construction company and keeps dozens of employees on their toes becomes a total weenie when it comes time to clean anything yucky off our kids or be in close proximity to remnants of bodily functions.

I also learned a lot about myself. My self-realization was hard to swallow: I'm not the fun one. I'm the one who schedules the fun, buys the fun, sets up the fun, makes snacks for the fun, tends to the boo-boos caused by the fun, and cleans up the debris from the fun, but I'm not the fun one. No matter how hard I try to be the fun one, my husband has claimed that role. I suppose it's tough to be considered the fun one when you're the parent who takes the kids to the doctor and the dentist, makes sure they do their homework, puts them in time-out for hitting each other, makes them wash all body parts with soap, refuses to negotiate on teeth brushing, insists that they say "please" and "thank you," buys clothes they don't want, informs them that it's not amusing to make farting noises, and then, to top it off, expects them to eat broccoli. When Dad is in charge of dinner, it's pizza. When Dad is in charge of bedtime, it's whenever the movie is over. When Dad is in charge of bathing, soap is optional. As for farting . . . need I say more? Of course, he's the fun one.

For Scott, becoming a parent provided him with an opportunity for a second childhood. For me, it became an opportunity to become a nurse, cook, chauffeur, teacher, negotiator, prison warden, and, of course, maid. When the Bennetts go out as a family, our roles are clearly defined. Scott is in charge of the fun, and I'm in charge of the trips to the restroom.

My children's school holds an annual Fall Festival. It's a day filled with inflatable slides, pony rides, games, food, auctions, and, hopefully, lots of money raised for the school.

The first year we attended, everyone was looking forward to the event—that is, everyone but me. Having to keep track of a five-year-old and a three-year-old in a crowded outdoor area is never fun. My husband was planning to come along, and one would think we'd work together to keep track of our kids. But my husband, a wonderful provider, a loyal and loving man, and my best friend, turns into an eight-year-old whenever he's within a mile of games, rides, or other types of fun meant for the under-12 crowd. So basically, my day was going to be spent keeping track of two young children and one overgrown child.

Added to my joy was the fact that it was 92 degrees and the entire event was held in the sun. My post-menopausal, hormonal evil twin was going to attempt to make many appearances throughout the day, so I knew I'd have to bite my tongue and act as if I enjoyed holding the camera, water bottles, leftover cotton candy, melting ice cream cones, sunscreen, and extra hats—all the while being sure to not miss any photo opportunities as my family raced off in three different directions. Thankfully, Fall Festival comes only once a year.

Our day started out at the small inflatable slide. My kids could hardly contain their excitement as they stood on the line. My husband was just as excited. As for me, I hadn't been out of the air-conditioned car for 20 minutes and was already a sweaty mess.

Technically, the slide was not built for adults, especially larger adults. It was a slide intended for children. All the adults present understood that concept without having to be told—that is, until Scott came along. He wanted to go down the slide. His first approach was to play the concerned parent and ask my son, Jack, about whether he was too nervous to go down alone and would he like Daddy to go with him.

"I can do it myself, Daddy," Jack insisted. Scott then turned to Gracie, but she shook her head. She didn't want to go with Daddy either. Normally, you could count on one of my kids to chicken out at the last minute after standing on a long line for a ride. But that time, it seemed that all the talks we'd had about confidence had paid off: much to my husband's disappointment, my two kids wanted to brave the slide on their own. If Scott couldn't go on the slide under the guise of helping one of his children, he'd have to move on to the children of strangers.

He heard a child in the line ahead of us tell his mother that he was afraid of the slide. "Jordan, you have to go by yourself because Mommy's afraid of heights," the woman told her son.

That was all my husband needed to hear. Like a lion suddenly sensing the scent of a gazelle, he snapped his head around. Opportunity stood right there—all 32 inches of it.

"I'll be happy to take your son down the slide," said my ever-selfless husband.

"Jordan, is that okay with you?" The woman asked her son. He nodded, and Scott was elated. Victory! He'd get to go on the slide.

But then the volunteer attendant in charge of the slide shook her head and informed Scott that it really wasn't made for adults. Scott looked at her and then pointed to the little boy as if to say she would be responsible for denying this child his moment of fun. She caved. Scott and little Jordan were next in line to go down the slide.

As Jordan approached the slide, he'd seen all the kids before him squealing with delight and must have come to the realization that it would be more fun without an adult. He told my husband that he wanted to go alone. Scott was crushed.

With no other children on the line in need of a slide escort, Scott was starting to worry. How would he get to go on the slide?

"Scott, this is a ride for children," I whispered, attempting to reason with him. We were new to the school and I had been working hard to make friends. I didn't want to have Gracie and Jack embarrassed by their parents so soon in the school year. "Do you really have to go on the slide?"

"Yes! I want to. It's a big slide, it can hold me," he responded.

Now, I'm sure there are mothers who have walked away from their tantrum-throwing children in supermarkets and pretended not to know them. As for me, it's my husband whom I inch away from when he becomes a ten-year-old with a driver's license. I casually found my way to the other side of the slide and began taking pictures of children I didn't know so no one would think that I was with him.

As Scott prepared to go down the slide, I stood on the other side and continued to take pictures. I heard other adults giggle at the sight of a grown man climbing the steps to the slide; I didn't dare look in Scott's direction for fear he'd call my name. I just hoped the slide would hold him. If it collapsed, my plan was to grab my two kids and head for the car. By the time Scott found his way out of all that deflated rubber, we'd be halfway home.

I held my breath as Scott reached the top of the slide. Although I swear I heard the compressor groan as it struggled to maintain its inflation, Scott made it safely down. As he exited, I whispered, "Okay, you've had your fun, now let's move on."

"I want to do it again," he said.

Old Habits Die Hard

By Kae

It never ceases to amaze me when I see little children bopping through a parking lot with not one adult paying them a lick of attention. I know that all mothers have their paranoias—just ask Pam! And I know that until now in this book, I may have seemed a little laissez faire. But let me assure you, I had plenty of parenting paranoias of my own. One of them was holding the kids' hands.

David and I had been having an ongoing battle over holding Matthew's hand. I was obsessed with ensuring that I never put Matthew in a position to be abducted in public. This is a theme that played out throughout the raising of my children. I was always concerned about where they were and whether they could be abducted if I wasn't being diligent about their safety. Crazy, you may ask? Maybe a little, but at least all my children reached adulthood being raised by their original parents.

When Matthew was little, David thought I was just an overprotective nut—until the carpet-shopping day. We had just purchased our first house and decided to go shopping for a rug for our dining room. Our young family trudged from store to store in a large shopping mall looking for exactly the right rug.

Finally we found the perfect one. I sat down with the salesman to fill out the paperwork while David watched Matthew. All day we had been arguing about holding Matthew's hand: David didn't understand why it was so important. As long as he could see Mathew that was safe enough for him. But he was about to find out that shopping in a crowded store with a young child can quickly turn into a harrowing experience for parents.

The rug area of the store had several tall, round racks from which various decorative rugs and cloths were hanging. While I at the salesman's desk, I suddenly heard David call out to Matthew in a panicked tone of voice. Immediately, I knew Matthew had gone missing. I jumped up. David, the salesman, and I searched for Matthew in the store's rug area. Just about the time real panic set in, we heard giggling come from under one of the racks. Pulling back the hanging cloths, we found Matthew playing hide and seek. I was relieved. David was devastated. He had inadvertently put his son in harm's way. I never again had to ask David to make sure to hold the kids' hands in public.

As I mentioned before, this need to hold my children's hands was an obsession. I just knew that if I didn't hold their hands the entire time we were in a parking lot, a wayward car would zoom into the unattended child, crushing him or her under its massive weight. As my kids got older, there were several instances where they didn't want to hold my hand. I quickly remedied this situation by informing them that if my hand was unoccupied I would instantly apply it to someone's backside. My strategy worked: The kids were more than happy to make sure my hand was occupied by holding onto theirs.

Even now that all my kids are grown and gone, when I babysit younger children and am out with them in public I always tell them they have to hold my hand the whole time. When they ask me why, I tell them, "I'm afraid I might get lost. Then I would be scared and would cry big alligator tears. Wouldn't that be terrible?" I have never had a kid balk at holding my hand when they think I am the one who might be lost and afraid.

Stopping the hand holding was traumatic for me. Slowly, each child got too old, but luckily I had Christina, who let me hold her hand in public for years after the average child would have been embarrassed. For me, old habits and paranoid thoughts die hard. One day when Matthew was 13 years old, he and I were about to cross a busy intersection together. Without thinking about it, I reached out for his hand. "Mom, what are you doing?" he asked indignantly. "You can't hold my hand to cross the street. I'm taller than you are!"

The funny thing is, each of my kids has mentioned to me how it drives them nuts to see a parent walking with a small child who is not holding their hand. My kids always turn to me and say, "Don't they know how dangerous that is?"

Earth to Pam

By Pam

When it came time to introduce solid foods to Gracie, I was determined to do it by the book—actually, by the dozens of books I had read about motherhood. My newly blossoming maternal instincts were telling me that this was an opportunity to start my baby off in the best possible way. Instead of buying baby food at the store, I thought, why not make my own? How hard could it be to puree peas and sweet potatoes? Yes, I would buy fresh vegetables and fruits and prepare them myself so I could ensure my precious child would get nothing but the best. If not for my fatal allergy to bees and lack of a green thumb, I might have also attempted to grow my own vegetables. Instead, I made the wise choice to shop for produce.

As if I didn't have enough baby books, I went to the store to buy yet another: This one was about making your own baby food. I bought plenty of ice cube trays, too, so I could freeze the food in single-serving sizes. I was going to be Earth Mother.

I began my first attempt at homemade baby food. I cooked some butternut squash, pureed it in the blender, then meticulously dropped equal amounts into each compartment of the ice cube trays. I placed the trays in my freezer until the food was hard enough to be put in plastic freezer bags that then had all the air sucked out of them with my trusty (but frighteningly noisy) FoodSaver vacuum sealer. I then moved on to the peas. All went well, and within a few hours I had a generous supply of frozen squash and peas that were labeled, dated, and stored.

In keeping with my need to schedule, clean, coordinate, worry, and over-complicate things, I put a calendar on the refrigerator so I could record which foods I had fed to Gracie. I also kept a list of the foods that still needed to be introduced and placed them in the order recommended by several baby books. We would be going from veggies to fruits to meats. Pureeing the veggies was relatively easy, but I was a bit concerned about how appetizing it was going to be when I had to stick chicken or beef in my food processor and grind it into a paste.

I followed the routine of feeding Gracie the same food for three days before moving on to another food, so I could identify any food allergies. Every couple of days I made a batch of a new vegetable. The first week was wonderful. I truly felt as if I was starting my child off with the best nutrition. Then week two hit and reality set in.

I am self-employed. I work as a certified cat behavior consultant. I travel to my clients' homes to do house calls. I also write books on cat behavior, speak at conferences, and do media appearances. At the time, I was also the spokesperson for a major cat food company and was required to go on tour for days at a time. Suddenly, my Suzy Homemaker schedule was in jeopardy.

Being out of town on business and traveling to client consultations when in town were starting to threaten my baby food production schedule. I now had to make baby food late at night, and since I didn't want to wake up Gracie, I took the blender full of food into the garage, where I plugged it in and pureed away. It was becoming less fun to be Earth Mother.

Then I received a packet of coupons in the mail from our supermarket. In the packet were pictures of happy, well-rested mothers feeding their content, well-nourished babies commercial baby food. I began thinking about all the babies who are fed baby food from jars. They all still grow up looking adequately nourished. Surely it must be okay. Well, I thought, it might be a good idea just to have a few jars on hand for emergencies. I gathered up Gracie and off we went to stock up on a few basics.

While in the baby food aisle, armed with my coupons, I thought of all the nights I carried the blender into the garage. I thought of all the ice cube trays perilously balanced in the freezer. I thought of all the times I forgot to thaw a particular food in time for the meal. Then suddenly, right there in the store, I saw beautiful, neat rows of jarred food glistening under the fluorescent light. Label after label faced me with pictures of happy, content, well-fed babies.

My plan to purchase a few jars for emergencies quickly became a quest to fill the bottom of my cart with every jar on the shelf. Squash, peas, carrots, chicken, turkey, sweet potato—you name it, it landed in my cart. I felt free yet terribly guilty.

At home, I emptied one of my kitchen cabinets and refilled it with stacks of baby food jars. Someone else would have to be the Earth Mother of the neighborhood. My blender was going back to making smoothies.

I also went into Gracie's room and took out the packages of cloth diapers I had recently bought. I faced the reality that I would probably never switch her over from disposables. The lure of Pampers convenience was just too strong. My Earth Mother had withered on the vine.

For years later, I remained conflicted about being Earth Mother. If you were to examine the contents of my shopping cart during those early times, you'd discover that Earth Mother-wannabe Pam would buy a fair amount of organic foods, but underneath them in the cart you'd also find Fruit Roll-Ups, Oreos, Doritos, and Cap'n Crunch. Happily though, I did come full circle back around and our family now eats all organic food. These days, when my children come to the dinner table you can pretty much count on one of them asking if we're going to have to eat healthy forever.

Just last night when I placed his dinner before him of organic chicken, organic green beans, and an organic sweet potato, Jack looked up at me with those beautiful brown eyes of his and said, "This healthy eating is going to KILL me."

Chapter 2

Discipline is Not for Sissies

One More Kiss

By Kae

The night Christina was born, she was brought back to me from the nursery at the hospital because she was crying so much that she was disturbing the other babies. As long as she was in the room with me, she was happy as a clam. The same was true when I took her home. She was a content and happy baby as long as I was in the room with her. As the days, weeks, and months went by, a pattern began to develop. If another adult touched Christina, she began to cry. If I took her to the doctor, she would be perfectly fine until the nurse came in the room and reached out and touched her. It was Mommy or nothing.

That fall, I returned to college. The first semester I attended night classes so that David and I could save money on the daycare bills. My class schedule was such that I had to leave the house about an hour before David got off the train. A girl who lived down the street and who babysat for many of the neighborhood kids come to our house and watched Matthew and Christina until David came home.

I have always been really careful not to encourage any of Christina's separation anxiety behavior. When she began crying with other people, I made a point to have someone else hold her if we were visiting friends or family. When we left the kids with a sitter, I would simply pick up my keys, tell the kids goodbye, and walk out the door. No long, drawn-out "parting is such sweet sorrow" scenes. Just out the door.

When my classes started, Christina would go to the door, sit in the entryway, and cry inconsolably until David came home. David would then pick her up, get her ready for bed, and put her to sleep. Although she would eventually stop crying when David came home, she was never quite happy. Because of Christina's crying, I ended up having to pay the sitter double to keep coming back.

When Christina was two, I decided to go back to school full time. Matthew and Christina were signed up at the daycare center. Matthew was excited to get back to his classroom and friends. Christina was completely unimpressed. The first day of daycare, I dropped the kids off and went back to the house. I didn't have class yet but wanted them to get used to going every day. About two hours later I got a phone call from the daycare. I had to pick Christina up immediately. She had broken out in welts all over her body.

I immediately called the doctor's office and got an emergency appointment. When I got to the school to pick her up, I was shocked. She had welts the size of goose eggs on her face. Her eyes were swollen slits. Her lips were swollen and red. I pulled up her shirt and her belly was covered in huge, angry red lumps. I snatched her up and off we ran in a panic to the doctor's office.

In the examination room I stripped her down to her diaper. She had huge welts everywhere. They were even on the palms of her hands and the soles of her feet. She was weeping and miserable. When the nurse came in, Christina began to cry in earnest. The nurse took a history of what she had eaten the day before and so far this day. She asked if we had changed laundry soap or bath soap. The answer was no. I am allergic to so many things that we never changed soaps.

The doctor finally came in, and through Christina's shrieking gave her a thorough examination. I explained that she was fine when I dropped her off at daycare. Also that this was her first day and she was sobbing when I left, and according to the daycare teacher, the crying didn't stop until I came in the room to pick her up. The doctor's diagnosis was that Christina had gotten herself so worked up that she had broken out in hives. To test her theory, the doctor gave me a sample dose of an antihistamine, but instructed me not to give it to Christina unless the hives had not gone down by bedtime. I was to take her home and continue with my regular day and simply watch her. I was to call the office if the hives appeared to be getting worse, but otherwise I should just call in the morning and let them know what happened.

Christina stopped crying as soon as the doctor closed the door to the exam room. I got her dressed and home we went. She spent the rest of the day playing, napping, and snacking just like every other day before she'd gone to daycare. When it was time to pick up Matthew, she went into the daycare happy as a clam and led me to Matthew's room. We went home and sure enough, by dinnertime her hives were completely gone. By the time David got home from work, there was not a sign of the angry red welts that had covered our daughter from head to foot.

I changed my class schedule so Christina would only have to go to daycare two days a week. We lingered around the daycare on the days that Matthew went and eventually I was able to leave without her breaking out in angry red hives. She still cried, though. I have to credit the patience of the teachers in her class. They treated her with love and concern but kept her actively engaged in the class activities and playing with the other children. She continued to go to daycare weepy but hive-free.

In the fall of 1989 we moved to a small town south of Nashville, Tennessee. Matthew began kindergarten and Christina and Jessica stayed at home with Mommy and Daddy. David had given up his job at one of the top law firms in the nation: We set up offices in our home and David opened his own securities law practice. He was a full-time stay-at-home dad for the first time in his life.

At this point, it is important for me to share some vital information. David was and always will be a better mother than I ever was. He is full of hugs and cuddles for the kids. He spent hours having tea parties with Christina while bouncing baby Jessica on one knee. He took the kids to the library and the park. He read them stories every night before they went to bed. David never shied away from any of the yucky stuff, either. He gave baths, changed diapers (even the toxic ones), kissed boo boos, and cleaned up more than his fair share of vomit. While David was wonderful at all these parenting roles, he was awful with discipline. If a child was distressed, David would walk on water to make him or her happy. Even if it meant incurring the Wrath of Mom.

One year before Christina was due to go to kindergarten, I enrolled her in preschool—with memories of angry red welts and sobbing fits racing in my mind. It was everything I had envisioned. She'd had a year at home with Mommy all day every day. We didn't have many babysitters because we were both home all the time. When I went back to school to finish my degree at night, David was home taking care of the kids.

After one rough start, we finally found a preschool where Christina thrived. The teachers in her class were young and vibrant. The lessons were designed to get the children ready to go to kindergarten. Our only hurdle was getting Christina to stop crying every morning when I left her.

She started out going to preschool two days a week. When I dropped her off, I made a point of giving her one hug and one kiss. Then I would turn around and leave the building, even if I could hear her crying from the parking lot and see her face pressed against the door. Every day when I picked her up I'd say, "See, I came back to pick you up again. What's all this crying for?"

After a few weeks the crying slowed to weeping. She knew I was going to drop her off and then be back in the afternoon to pick her up. At this pace, things were on track for a crying-free kindergarten the following year.

Finally, Christina graduated to attending preschool five days a week. I had joined a bowling league and began to have a ladies' late night out with some of my bowling friends. One day a week, David took over the routine of getting the kids up, dressed, fed, and off to school. On his first day, he dropped Matthew off at school and took Christina to preschool. Entering the building, Christina began to cry. Seeing his child in distress, David panicked. She looked up at him with her large blue, tear-filled eyes and begged, "Please Daddy, if I can give my mommy one more kiss, I'll go to school." So back in the car they went. I was jostled awake to find a gleeful Christina jumping on my bed.

It made me furious with David. I had spent all this time and effort establishing the tough love drop-off method, and in one day he had potentially reversed all my hard work. I slammed out of bed, threw on some clothes, and brushed my hair. Then I put Christina back in the car and drove her back to preschool. On the way, I lectured her. "Young lady, this is the last time you are ever going to pull this kind of stunt, do you understand me?"

"Yes, ma'am." Christina looked truly ashamed of herself.

"What were you thinking?" I asked her.

"I just wanted to give you one more kiss."

"You can give me kisses when you come home from school."

"Yes, Mommy."

"You have gotten your father into big trouble, did you know that? I am really angry about this."

"Don't get Daddy in trouble. I won't do it again, I promise." She pleaded to save her father from being flogged by her angry mommy.

I pulled into the parking lot of the preschool and put the car in Park. "You listen to me, young lady. I have had enough of this," I said to Christina as I switched off the car and turned in my seat to face her. "Have I ever left you at school?"

"No."

"Have you ever had to get one of your teachers to drive you home after it got dark because I forgot to get you?"

"No."

"Don't I show up at the same time every day?"

"Yes."

"Then if I have never left you here overnight and I pick you up at the same time every day, what is there for you to cry about?"

"Cause I miss you," Christina said with her big blue eyes beginning to mist up.

"I miss you too, but I know how happy I will be to see you when I pick you up and that makes it okay." I took Christina's hand in mine. "Now, young lady, you are going to march yourself into that preschool and apologize to your teacher for being bad this morning, do you understand me?"

"Yes."

"Then I am going to give you one hug and one kiss. Do you understand me?"

"Yes."

I took Christina into the preschool and delivered her into the care of her teacher. Christina apologized for being bad earlier. I gave her one hug and one kiss. To her credit, I never heard her cry that day when I walked out the door.

A normal person would think the argument David and I had when I got home, coupled with the talking-to that Christina had received on her way to school, would have resolved this situation. But in case you haven't noticed, our family is not normal. Once a week for the next several months, David brought Christina to school, put her back in the car at the first sign of distress, and brought her back home. I would then put her directly back into the car and lecture her all the way back to the preschool.

By some miracle, just before kindergarten started, she outgrew crying when David or I left her at school. I was elated. The first day of kindergarten, I walked her to her room, full of fear that she would start to cry in front of her new classmates and they would make fun of her for being a baby. But she waltzed right into the room, big as you please. That night at dinner she surprised me by telling about how some of the other kids in her class had cried when their mommies left, but she didn't make fun of them because she knew how they felt.

Thirteen years later, we drove four and a half hours away to drop Christina off at college. It was one of the hardest things her daddy and I ever had to do. Standing in the parking lot, tears streaming down her face, she hugged her father and said, "Daddy, if I can get one more hug I'll go to college."

The Pajama Game

By Pam

There was a brief time, when Gracie was four and Jack was two, when I was starting to feel as if the balance of power was in my favor and I was actually doing okay in the mothering department. Gracie had passed the terrible twos and the even-worse threes, and was becoming a cooperative, well-behaved child. Jack had entered the twos, but so far hadn't been showing any signs of being terrible, so I was enjoying the quiet, well-mannered children inhabiting my home. Oh, don't get me wrong, I wasn't that naive—I knew I was living on borrowed time and Jack's temperament could change in the blink of an eye. But I was happy for the time being. I took advantage of this calm before the storm to have family dinners in public restaurants, take my kids grocery shopping, visit the zoo, and even the library. It was nice while it lasted.

The calm was broken not by Jack recognizing that he needed to live up to the terrible twos, but rather by Gracie. She came to the realization that although she had to submit to adult authority when it came to manners, nutrition, and bedtime, there was absolutely no reason to have an adult tell her what she should wear. At four, Gracie determined that she should be in control of her fashion destiny.

This resulted in me having to spend time explaining to my daughter why she couldn't wear her Halloween costume to preschool when it wasn't Halloween. And of course, we certainly had our share of heart-to-heart discussions on why pajamas weren't meant to be school clothes. I was managing to win this war with just a few minor concessions (such as allowing her to wear her underwear inside out or her pants on backwards), but I wasn't expecting the preschool itself to cross over to the enemy side.

We had survived five mornings in a row of Gracie being willing to make fashion compromises without so much as a sniffle or a pouting lip. She understood which clothes were for inside the house and which clothes were for school, church, and play. She was starting to lose interest in insisting on wearing underpants around her neck or attaching toilet paper to her belt loops. I was beginning to think I had dodged a bullet, based on the horror stories I'd heard from friends. Then the rules changed. I went to Gracie's preschool on Friday afternoon to pick her up and there was a note in her cubby from the teacher. The note happily announced that Monday would be "pajama day" and everyone was to wear their favorite PJs to school.

After weeks of explaining to my children that one doesn't go to school in pajamas, I now had to tell them that in this case, it was okay to wear pajamas.

"No Mommy, I can't," Gracie said as she shoved the pajamas away.

My son, who attended the same preschool, had jumped at the chance to not have to get dressed for school. Being the typical boy, he didn't pay the least bit of attention to his attire and often wasn't even aware of whether he was actually wearing any clothes or not. I frequently had to remind him that he had left his underwear and pants in the bathroom after going potty.

"Gracie, this is a special and fun day and all the kids will be wearing pajamas," I replied while holding the pajamas up enticingly.

"We don't wear our pajamas out of the house. All the kids will laugh," she said. Jack looked at her in confusion and then looked back at me. He certainly wanted to wear his pajamas outside, but if this was a trick, he wasn't about to fall for it. He often depended on his older sister to protect him from bad toddler decisions.

I shook my head, "No, they won't, honey. All the kids will be wearing pajamas as well. It's just for fun. "

Gracie shook her head and folded her arms across her chest in that way children do that tells every mother there will be no more discussion on the subject. Jack's lower lip started to extend into its usual pout, and he began to slowly pull his pajamas bottoms down. I reached over and touched his hand and shook my head. "Jack, this is a special day. I promise you can wear your pajamas on this day only, okay?" I smiled. He smiled back and nodded.

Then he shot a quick glance over to Gracie for confirmation, but she was busy kicking the pajamas off into the corner.

"I tell you what," I continued, despite the threat of a tantrum in the air, "I'll wear my pajamas when I take you to school."

"No!" Gracie replied in what I can only describe as disgust.

So we each went to our separate bedrooms and prepared for school. Gracie chose a totally appropriate school outfit of pretty pink pants and a pink striped top, and I chose my red flannel pajamas with white snowflakes. Jack had on his favorite dinosaur pajamas. Gracie didn't talk to me during the entire ride to school.

When we arrived at the school parking lot, she saw the other kids getting out of the cars wearing . . . you guessed it . . . pajamas! Jack started clapping and laughing.

"Mommy, look!" Gracie wailed as she pointed to a classmate wearing Mickey Mouse pajamas. "I'm gonna' look silly in my clothes."

That's when pajama-clad Smart Mommy went into action. I opened my purse and pulled out a pair of Gracie's pink flowered pajamas—her favorites. I helped Gracie do a quick change into her pajamas in the back of the minivan and then the three of us walked hand in hand into the preschool. I was happy because I stupidly thought I had outsmarted my four-year-old. Gracie was happy because she was sure I didn't know what I was talking about when it came to fashion logic. And Jack was happy because he didn't care what he was wearing.

Unfortunately, the fun of pajama day had a lingering negative effect on my attempts at teaching fashion appropriateness to my daughter. The very next morning, Gracie walked out of her room already dressed for preschool. Her decision to cover the bases and dress for all seasons was nothing short of inspiring, I have to admit. She started off with her purple winter cap with the pom-pom on top. Of course the pom-pom didn't sufficiently complete the look of the hat, so Gracie added the extra touch of her Cinderella crown. The crown did have purple gems around it, so I had to give her credit for color matching. Moving on down the body, she had on her purple and green one-piece bathing suit. Not just any bathing suit, mind you, but the one with the Styrofoam inserts for beginning swimmers. It made her look as if she was wearing an armor chest plate. And no bathing suit would be complete without insulated pink snow pants. I knew they were a favorite of Gracie's because she liked the way they swished when she walked. For a preschooler, sound plays an important part in fashion. Finally, Gracie's feet were shod in Jack's Thomas the Tank Engine shoes. They were a full size too small for her feet.

"Why are you wearing Jack's shoes, Gracie?" I asked. There were so many questions on my mind regarding her choice of attire, but the ill-fitting shoes seemed to take priority.

"They light up and mine don't. I want to make sure the kids see me," she responded, and tapped one foot on the floor to make it blink for emphasis.

"And you think they won't notice you in this outfit unless your shoes are blinking?" I giggled, and then caught myself when I saw the look of indignation on Gracie's face.

I was unsure just where to begin. "Gracie honey, first of all, those shoes are too small for you. Don't they hurt your feet?"

"I made my toes smaller."

Of course, a logical answer coming from a four-year-old. "How did you make your toes smaller?" I had to ask.

"I keep them bent," she replied, as if everybody should know that.

"Regardless of how small you make your toes, you can't wear Jack's shoes. You also can't wear your bathing suit to school."

"I want to wear my bathing suit!" she announced and put her hands on her hips, but had trouble keeping them there because of the slippery nylon of the snow pants. "You said we couldn't wear pajamas but we all did!"

"Gracie," I said in my Mommy's-Getting-Angry voice.

"This is what I'm wearing!" she said firmly, and then spun around and went back to her room swishing and blinking the entire way.

I let her wear her unique outfit during breakfast but then convinced her to change into regular school clothes before we had to leave. I compromised by letting her wear her bathing suit under her clothes (minus the Styrofoam pads).

The preschool fashion war is tough. Sometimes you win and sometimes you want to pin a sign on your child that says "I dressed myself" to make sure everyone knows you had nothing to do with this.

Not in Indiana

By Kae

After we moved to Tennessee, the Christmas holidays found the Allen family on the road to Chicago. The family tradition was to have Christmas with David's parents. This was a nine-hour drive, door to door. We had a station wagon with a jump seat in the back, and we always stuck a luggage carrier on the top of the car. Jessica, in her car seat, sat in the middle of the back seat, with the extra luggage and Christmas presents filling the space on either side. Matthew and Christina sat in the jump seat in the back. David was the driver; I was the co-pilot.

The drive always went well in the first few hours. The kids were excited about going on a trip. Matthew and Christina sat in the jump seat making up stories about driving an 18-wheeler or flying to the moon in a spaceship. They always enjoyed the game of pumping their arms in the windows to get the truck drivers to blow their horns.

About an hour and a half into the trip, we crossed the Kentucky state line. David honked the horn and we all cheered, "Yeah, Kentucky." Two hours later, we were in Indiana. Once again David honked the horn as we crossed the Indiana state line, and we all cheered, "Yeah, Indiana."

This was where the time always began to drag. Half the trip was spent in Indiana. By then, the kids had usually lost interest in the fantasy they were playing out; plus, the landscape was flat and boring. This is when the trouble predictably began. Matthew and Christina started to feel cramped in the little jump seat area. Invariably, Matthew began to subtly pick on Christina by taking his shoes off and threatening to put his feet on or near her. Christina has always had a thing about feet. She doesn't want anyone's feet near her, and she especially doesn't want anyone to touch her feet.

If the feet didn't get her going, Matthew was the resident expert when it came to farting on command. He'd figured out a way to raise his butt up on the seat so that it was pointing at Christina, and then he let it rip. As he no doubt knew, this was guaranteed to get a shriek out of Christina, followed by, "Mommy, Matthew is farting on me."

"Matthew cut it out," I'd command from the front seat.

So Matthew then exploited the technicality that my command left open by taking Christina's pillow, tucking it under his butt, and letting one fly. After all, it wasn't directly on Christina.

Christina's shriek was followed by, "Mommy, Matthew farted on my pillow."

"Matthew, I said to cut it out, and I mean now," I said again, starting to get irritated.

Then Christina, feeling that she did not get sufficient retribution from me, began covertly picking at Matthew. She took his cars and pushed his bag of toys onto the floor. Matthew yelled, "Mommy, Steenie's (his nickname for her) touching my stuff."

And this was pretty much how the spiral into the sibling pissing war always began, give or take minor variations. After about five minutes of this, I was past my toleration level. "I swear, if you two don't cut it out I will come back there and bop you both in the head."

This was always followed by David's standard line, "Don't bop the kids."

Once the kids heard this, it was usually gloves off. As far as they were concerned, Daddy would save them from getting bopped on the head so the slugfest was on in earnest.

As for me, after I issued the warning, that was it. This was such a common occurrence on our trips that the click of my seat belt being undone signaled all the kids to duck. Jessica dropped her head onto the padded lap bar of her car seat and wrapped her arms around her head. From the front seat I dove through the opening between the driver and passenger's seats. I flew over the top of Jessica's car seat, stretching as far as I could into the back of the car.

When I was in this position, David began to swerve the car back and forth. Since I was basically balancing on top of Jessica's car seat in the Superman pose, the small swerving motion sent my body flopping back and forth. This effectively made bopping the kids on the head somewhat like hitting moving targets at a carnival duck shoot. Matthew and Christina assumed the "this plane is going down" position so their heads were as far away from my flapping hands as possible. Eventually, I managed to give each of them a bop on the head and tell them I would come back there again if they didn't cut it out. This usually put a squash on the squabbling, at least for a little while.

One trip, the kids were being particularly hateful to each other. I had already done the car swerve bop, but they kept it up. This called for drastic measures.

"If you two don't cut it out I swear I'm going to put you out of this car," I said in my annoyed voice.

"You can't put us out of the car because Daddy won't stop the car," Matthew informed me in his wiseacre tone.

"We don't have to stop, Mr. Smarty Pants. I'll just throw you out the window while the car is moving."

"You can't do that; it's illegal," Matthew said authoritatively.

"Not in Indiana," I said in a dead serious tone of voice.

Believe it or not, that was it. The kids quit fighting and rode along like little angels. Every hour or so they would ask, "Are we still in Indiana?"

For several years after that, the kids were firmly convinced that it was perfectly legal in the state of Indiana for bad children to be thrown from moving cars. I was always assured that when we crossed from Kentucky into Indiana and we honked the horn and cheered, the kids would behave themselves for the rest of the trip.

When my son was 23, he and I drove to his grandparents' home for the weekend. We had a big laugh when Matthew, driving the car, crossed the Indiana state line and honked the horn. He looked at me with a glimmer in his eyes, then gestured toward the window. "Mom, you'd better be good."

Who's the Parent Here

By Pam

Discipline was a major concern for me when I started thinking about how I would teach my children to behave. After all, when your children reach a certain age, wagging your finger at them and saying, "That's a no-no" no longer has the same effect. It was time to step up the discipline. And being the marshmallow mother I knew I was, I had to have a good plan.

Scott and I were both raised in families that believed a good spanking solved everything. We both agreed that was not the approach for us, so I headed for the bookstore to read everything I could from the experts on how to effectively discipline children. Instead of getting answers, I got a headache. It seemed that for every expert who said spanking was wrong, another one said it was the good, old-fashioned way to go. Then there were the experts who said you should talk problems out with your children and explain at that moment why you didn't like their behavior. How do you communicate with a screaming, tantrum-throwing three-year-old that his behavior is less than polite?

After polling all the mothers I knew and reading dog-eared books in Kae's library on How to Solve a Child's Problem Behavior in 30 Seconds or Less, I came to the conclusion that time-out seemed to make the most sense. It was the most logical solution: quickly and calmly removing the misbehaving child from the scene of the crime. Of course, I then learned that time-out was not as simple as it seemed. Were you supposed to put your child in time-out in his room? Some experts claimed that was like punishing a child by letting him go to Disneyland. What about putting him in the corner? Should time-out take place where you can watch him? Then there was the popular television nanny's technique of the "naughty mat" that you sit your child on.

Since I knew my children better than anyone, I believed the worst punishment they could endure was quick removal from being the center of attention. Even though their rooms were filled with lots of fun toys, I knew they would hate being in there if everyone else was in another part of the house. My children thrived on having an audience. So I decided time-outs would take place in their respective bedrooms in official time-out chairs.

Next came the decision about the length of time-outs. Again, I recalled that many experts recommended time-out last one minute for every year of age. I had to giggle at that one, because in many cases, it took a good five minutes just for my kids to calm down in time-out. I couldn't imagine popping into their rooms while they were still in the middle of their toddler rantings to announce that time-out was over. That made no sense. With my kids, time-outs would last as long as it took them to calm down. With all due respect to the experts, I had to make my decisions under actual combat conditions. In a perfect world, a perfectly executed three-minute time-out might be wonderfully magical for a defiant, kicking, hitting, venom-spewing three-year-old child, but in my world, that wasn't going to cut it.

Now that we had decided punishments would consist of time-outs in their bedrooms, my next dilemma occurred the first time I tried to enforce this. Telling my defiant, kicking, hitting, venom-spewing child to go to time-out was like asking a grizzly bear to walk on tiptoes. So, I had to create Plan B. I decided to give my kids a choice, and the outcome would depend solely on decisions they would make themselves.

The choice was simple: You can go to time-out on your own and stay there for the assigned time, or Mommy will take you to time-out, and in that case, there will be an automatic toy removal tacked on to your punishment. Judging by the bug-eyed looks I received from my children at the mere mention of subtracting a toy from their collection, I had hit a punishment bull's-eye.

The first one to test me on this was Gracie. She had smart-mouthed me and was instructed to go to time-out. "No," she said, as she folded her arms across her chest and looked me right in the eye.

I could feel the fire rising up inside me and I remembered one of the experts in the parenting books who recommended to "parent without breaking a sweat." No matter how the child is acting, the parent is supposed to stay calm and composed, with no telltale beads of perspiration forming on the brow that might indicate to the child that a nerve had been hit. I took a deep breath, knelt down in front of Gracie, and quietly but firmly said, "You have two choices: go to time-out on your own or I will carry you there and you'll lose a toy for the rest of the day." I was rather pleased with myself for showing calm in the face of the storm. No beads of perspiration so far.

"I don't care," Gracie responded and stood her ground.

"Then you made your decision," I said and scooped her up in my arms. I carried her down the hall and into her room, where I seated her on her little chair and told her not to move. She quickly stood up, walked over to her toy shelves, and picked out a toy. She then walked over to me and surrendered it. Nice try, I thought, but I happen to know you don't like this toy very much.

"Gracie, I'm sorry, but Mommy is the one who picks out which toy will be taken away, not you."

"What?" she cried. Suddenly her neat little plan was backfiring. She thought she could con me with this old McDonald's Happy Meal toy when there were dolls, Cinderella slippers, and Hello Kitty stuffed animals in the vicinity. No way!

I put the Happy Meal toy back on her shelf and removed her Hello Kitty purse. She started crying. Bull's-eye! One thing I have little tolerance for is my children answering me back. "The purse will be returned to you tomorrow," I said in my Official Mommy voice. I motioned for her to sit in her chair. "Now I suggest you do your time-out and think about your behavior." With that, I tucked her fuzzy Hello Kitty purse under my arm and walked out of the room.

Time-outs are still a common method of punishment at our house, although I'm happy to report they occur less frequently. Sometimes though, they happen before the kids even have a chance to get out of their pajamas in the morning. Jack is an expert at what I call "revolving door time-outs." After he has finished the first time-out and is on his way out of his room, he mutters something under his breath or can't resist taking another verbal swing at Gracie, and so he is spun around on his heels and sent right back to the hot seat.

One unexpected benefit of time-out is that it tends to become a time of confession, and my kids end up spilling the beans about other things they've done. After a time-out, I go into my child's room, kneel down by the chair, and ask why Mommy had to put him or her in a time-out. I do this to make sure they understand why they were being punished. What sometimes happens, though, is that I get the bonus of hearing about other things they have done that I wasn't aware of—such as the time Gracie confessed that she was the one who put Barbie in the kitty litter box because she wanted her to have a day at the beach. No one had previously owned up to that. Then there was the time Jack offered the bonus confession of admitting he had given his giraffe a hair cut with Gracie's school scissors. Oh, and there was the post-time-out bonus confession from Gracie that both she and Jack had pulled my freshly planted petunias out of the ground. I had assumed it was a mole.

When Gracie was five-and-a-half, she created an adaptation of time-out. Whenever she got mad at me, she'd announce that she was going to sit in time-out and that I was no longer her best friend. I guess since she couldn't put me in time-out, putting herself in was the next best thing.

One aspect of time-out that has always been consistent in our home is that afterward, the culprit always gets a hug and kiss from Mommy and all is forgiven.

I know it won't be too long before time-outs advance into the teenage phase of grounding. I just hope grounding will have the same effect as time-out, and my kids will continue to offer those bonus confessions. Somehow, though, I doubt it.

Teach Your Child to Swim at Your Own Risk

By Kae

Every mother I have ever spoken to can recount, in intricate detail, the worst day of her maternal life. Mine was a certain day in February when Matthew was four years old.

Matthew's "holy terror" stage, as I lovingly refer to it, began that winter. It started with some whining and talking back. At first I thought this was just a stage he was going through. Or maybe he was simply getting four-years-old cabin fever because it had been so cold and snowy the past few weeks, and we hadn't been spending much time outdoors.

It escalated one day when I was putting the kids down for their naps. I put Christina in her bed and tucked her in. I went across the hall and walked into Matthew's room just in time to watch him whip out his fire hose (the name I assigned to a particular male body part) and pee in the corner of his room. I was shocked. "Matthew, what are you doing? You know better than that. Get in the bathroom." This was completely outside the normal pattern of his behavior. Since potty training—and all the warnings not to damage your child during the process—was still fresh in my mind, I decided not to discipline him. Maybe this was an isolated case of weirdness and would pass on its own.

Week by week, though, his behavior got worse and worse. He was spending a lot of time sitting on the edge of his bed with his hands folded in his lap and his head hung in shame. He was the recipient of several spankings. Then he ramped it up to the next level.

I was due to deliver Jessica any time in the next two weeks. When the kids went down for their nap, so did I. One day I woke up to the sound of someone softly snickering. I got up quietly and found Matthew huddled at the baby gate in front of Christina's room. When I walked into the hallway, Matthew beat a path back into his room and jumped into his bed. Not hearing any further noise, I went back to bed and finished my nap. When naptime was over, I went to Christina's room to get her up. I took the baby gate down and, without looking, started into the room. I felt something squish between my toes. Looking down, I was mortified to see a big pile of poop with my foot planted directly in the center. Taking in the whole scene, I followed a trail of poop across the beige carpet in a straight line through her room, with a crumpled-up diaper at the end of the line. "What the hell," I said as I tried to make sense of the scene before me. In the bed lay Christina with her poop-covered naked butt poking up in the air, sound asleep.

I woke Christina up and said, "This is a no, no. This is very bad," as I pointed out the poop streak in the carpet. I put Christina in the bathtub and washed her clean. Then I put Christina and Matthew together in Matthew's room with the baby gate in the doorway and told them, "Play nice while I clean up this mess." I got a bucket and filled it with hot soapy water and set to work on the carpet. Once again I chastised myself for not investing in those yellow rubber gloves that my grandmother always had under her kitchen sink. As the hot water soaked into the streak of poop on the carpet, something about the smell of the soap mixed with the poop started to make me gag. I threw up in my bucket of cleanup water.

After I went into the bathroom and cleaned the bucket out, I filled it with fresh water. Once again, I lowered my nine-months-pregnant-self onto the poop-defiled floor. It seemed like I spent hours scrubbing on my hands and knees trying to get the streak out of the beige carpet. The chore was made longer by my constant puking into the clean water and having to refill the bucket.

As bad as this was, it got worse the next day. And the next. And the day after that one, too. After a week of getting up from my nap every day with a pile of poop and a smear from Christina wiping her butt across the beige carpet, I decided to spy on the kids during naptime to find out exactly what was going on.

Sure enough, just after naptime started, Matthew crept across the hallway to Christina's door. There he sat, telling Christina, "Take your diaper off, Steenie. You can scoot on the carpet to get the dirt off your butt." All the while he was snickering.

"Matthew Russell, what the heck are you doing?" I roared as I came out of the bedroom like an enraged bull. "Get in your room right this second before I bust your butt." Matthew took off like a rocket into his room. "Christina Marie, don't you ever, ever, ever do this again," I said as I snatched Christina up from the end of the poop streak and put her into the bathtub. The next day was Saturday. David stayed home from work and was spending the day with the kids. When he went to get them up from their nap, he was eyewitness to the carnage I'd told him about all week. This was the first time I saw David lose his temper with Christina. He grabbed her up and put her stark naked into the empty bathtub until he finished scrubbing the poop out of the carpet. This may have been the last time Christina pulled off her diaper during naptime. She did not like being in trouble with her daddy.

But Matthew had been the instigator, and his behavior had deteriorated to a point where I was obsessed with trying to figure out why. This surely wasn't a normal phase every child goes through. At first I thought maybe he was angry about the new baby coming. We had just finished putting up the wallpaper in the new nursery, and I had spent a fair bit of time getting the room organized. But it didn't make sense that Matthew had been so happy about Christina's arrival, yet was so upset about the new baby. I'd heard about the terrible twos and the horrible threes, but I thought the fours were a time of respite for the parents who'd survived. I consulted the reference section of All the Goofy Advice About Babydom and found nothing that seemed to fit with Matthew's behavior.

I knew something was going on with him that was making him act out. I elicited advice from my mother-in-law and my friends with children. I went through Matthew's clothes to make sure I had removed all the scratchy tags. I talked to the teachers at this preschool and was told that he was having no problems at school. I was stymied.

The bottom of this spiral into parental hell came the night he "lost" a Matchbox car. David was working late, so I had fed the kids dinner, given them a bath, and gotten them ready for bed. Usually this was a quiet and peaceful time of snuggles and reading. This night it was chaos.

Matthew began by complaining about what we were having for dinner. This surprised me, because we were having chicken and dumplings, his all-time favorite. He started a big stink with Christina at dinner and had her in tears before the meal was over.

During their bath, Matthew intentionally splashed water all over Christina's face, launching her into shrieking fits of: "Water my eyes, water my eyes." When it came time to wash their hair, Matthew said, "Watch out Steenie, Mommy will put water in your face. This caused another round of shrieking from Christina.

I put her to bed while Matthew put on his pajamas, then sat on the edge of his bed with his hands folded in his lap and his head hung in shame. When I went in to put him to bed, he whined that he couldn't find a specific Matchbox car he wanted to sleep with. I looked under his bed—no easy feat for a pregnant woman ready to deliver at any moment. I looked all over his room and could not find the cherished car. I went back downstairs and looked in all the rooms. Meanwhile, he was in his bed upstairs, wailing that he wanted his car. I could not find it. He came downstairs, placed his little fists on his hips and told me, "Find my car right now," emphasizing his point with a stamp of his foot. This outburst was rewarded with a swat on the butt and him running for the cover of his bed sheets.

From the bedroom he wailed on and on. I told him I couldn't find the car and offered all the other cars I could find as replacements. He kept getting louder and louder. Finally, I told him to go to sleep and closed his door. Too tired to go back downstairs, I went in my bedroom and tried to read a book. I heard Matthew's bedroom door squeak open. He ran across the hallway and started calling to Christina. When she didn't answer, he threw a car at her bed and hit her square in the face. Christina began to wail.

Bolting out of my room, I startled him. "Get back in your bed right now!" I thundered. I climbed over the gate across the doorway of Christina's room and scooped her up in my arms. A few kisses on the ugly red mark on her cheek where the car had landed—followed by a back rub later—she was calm and drifted back to sleep. Then Matthew began screaming: "I want my car, I want my car."

I went to his doorway, not trusting myself to go in. I wanted nothing more than to blister his little butt red, but that was not listed in the All the Goofy Advice About Babydom books as being an acceptable discipline method, so I stayed in the hall. "Matthew," I said sharply, "you lie down and go to sleep this instant."

Okay, I'm a coward or a hero, depending on how you look at it. I'd had all that I could possibly take from the child. I was beginning to understand how a parent can just snap. I went back to my room and closed the door. Matthew continued his screaming about his car and took up kicking the wall apparently for emphasis.

The, the door opened to our bedroom and David walked in looking bewildered and exhausted from a long day at the office. "What's going on in here?"

That's when I began to cry—not a tiny little leaking of tears from my eyes, but great big, giant sobs. "Your son is driving me crazy. I want you to take him to the nearest orphanage and drop him off. I am dead serious David Russell. I want you to take that child out of here and don't bring him back." David looked stunned.

"Just tell me what's going on," he said as he closed the bedroom door.

I sobbed out the entire story of the evening, getting angrier and angrier with every word. He gave me a hug and said, "Let me talk to him; it will be okay." With that, David went across the hall to Matthew's room and explained to him that Mommy had looked everywhere for his Matchbox car and couldn't find it. It was time for bed and we would all look for it in the morning." Matthew responded in the sweet little voice that the child involved in this night of terror had not possessed, "Okay, Daddy. I love you."

David came back to the bedroom, pleased as punch with himself. "There you go sweetheart, everything is all worked out."

Now I was really pissed off. I had been through trial by fire with that kid for the past three hours and David merely waltzes in and the brat gives him the "Okay, Daddy, I love you" bit. I thought my head was going to explode. "You go get that boy up and take him out of here, do you understand me. It's either him or me. I have had it!" I thundered.

David came over, put his arms around me, and whispered soothing things in my ears until I finally admitted that taking Matthew to an orphanage in the middle of the night might not be a well-thought-out plan. Suddenly, to my surprise, the house was quiet.

David's solution, when you have an argument, is to make up and give everyone a hug whether they want it or not. So on this night he said to me, "Just go give Matthew a hug. It will be okay."

We went into Matthew's room. I sat on the edge of his bed and gazed at the angelic sleeping child. It was hard to believe the demon that had wreaked havoc on my peaceful home was the same sleeping child. Now I felt really guilty for wanting him dropped off at the nearest orphanage. He was my precious boy, and my heart swelled with love for him. I reached out and gathered him and his pillow into my arms, and my hand bumped up against something metal under his pillow. I kissed him on the cheek and laid him back down. I reached under the pillow and pulled out the metal object. To my astonishment, it was the Matchbox car he had been screaming for all night.

David, quickly reading the look on my face, dragged me out of the room before I could do something I'd regret.

As odd as it might sound, the next day Matthew began acting like his normal self. He was not a perfect angel, but he was not the holy terror he had been for the past few weeks.

That night has become a legend in our household. Although some legends get bigger with each retelling, this one has stayed fairly true to the events. It was a horrible night and Matthew remembers it only vaguely. What he does remember is doing all the things that lead up to the night. During one of our family legend-telling sessions, he finally enlightened me about why he acted so horribly, "I was mad at you because you put me in swim classes and the water made my thumb taste funny."

In retrospect, I realized that the end of the swim classes came the same week that Jessica was born. By the time I was home with the new baby, Matthew was back to normal. My advice to all the other mothers out there: Make sure your children have quit sucking their thumbs before you send them to swim lessons.

Tiny Locksmiths

By Pam

Like most mothers, when my first child became mobile, I was fanatically concerned with protecting her from the infinite dangers in my home. As a new mother, I stood in the baby safety section of the department store and loaded up my shopping cart with all the gadgets and gizmos that would protect my precious baby from harm. The packaging on objects led me to believe that my house was basically a death trap. I began to wonder how my nieces and nephews had survived previous visits to my home. Obviously, I had dodged numerous bullets. But I was not going to take any more chances.

First on my list was the toilet. I bought locks for every toilet in the house. I was impressed with how complicated they were and was sure no child would be able to fall in and drown. What I soon came to realize, though, was that these complicated toilet locks were not only childproof, they also were adult-proof. A specific order needed to be followed to free the toilet lid. One had to simultaneously squeeze two levers together while lifting the latch. It was a two-handed operation, and it took a fair amount of strength and coordination to accomplish. All guests to our home had to be given instructions regarding the toilet locks. It was inconvenient, and I'm sure several of our friends chose not to visit because it was too difficult to use our bathroom. Babysitters probably tried not to drink much liquid while at our house to limit how many times they'd have to wrestle with the toilet. But we didn't care that we were becoming increasingly unpopular. My baby daughter remained safe.

Toddlers are very strange little creatures. You don't think they're paying much attention to you—actually, you're convinced of it based on how many times you must repeat simple instructions—but they're really little video recording devices that observe with intensity. Silly me, I just assumed a little toddler wouldn't have the strength or the coordination to squeeze the toilet lock levers together while simultaneously lifting the latch. After all, if grown adults had trouble making it work, how in the world could a toddler manage?

That's where life shows its sense of humor. It lulls you into a false sense of security by giving you an infant, so you get used to being the one with the brains and brawn. Then your fragile little infant becomes a toddler and you enter into an alien world where nothing makes sense. Your two-year-old, the same one who can't hold a cup of milk without spilling it, can climb out of her crib, find your car keys in the middle of the night, and stand at the front door hitting the alarm button just to hear the blaring car horn. Yet you still naively think that installing flimsy plastic locks on cabinets, drawers, and toilets will deter the mighty toddler.

Gracie often watched as one of our guests entered the bathroom, having been given the detailed toilet-unlocking instructions, only to sheepishly return to the dining table to whisper in my ear that the toilet was still locked. Eventually, Gracie must've felt sorry for my guests, because when my mother went into the bathroom Gracie jumped up from her seat, ran in after her, and effortlessly unlocked the toilet for Grandma. The toilet lock that had taken my husband 20 minutes to install and had baffled every college-educated adult who entered our home was opened in seconds by my two-year-old.

At that point, I realized that instead of locking the toilet—which was, of course, only managing to keep the adults out of it anyway—I should assume my role as a mother and teach Gracie what does and doesn't belong in the toilet. Since I couldn't protect her from all the unlocked toilets we would encounter, it would be better to explain Toilet Safety 101.

She was quick to grasp the concept that heads and hands had no place in the toilet. But we did have a few setbacks when it came to other objects, such as magnetic alphabet letters, small blocks, a Dora the Explorer doll, and a handful of cat food. She also took awhile to understand how much toilet paper is too much to flush down the toilet. So yes, we did have our share of bathroom floods and Dora the Explorer will probably be forever swimming in our septic tank, but I'm happy to report that not once did I lose a child down the toilet.

Another interesting childproofing technique that we attempted was to lock drawers with magnetic locks. In theory, this is such a great concept. You install a magnet lock on the inside of the drawer that can only be opened with a magnetic key. The key is simply a smooth magnet you run across the corner of the drawer that releases the magnetic lock. I loved the idea because all the other drawer locks let the drawer be pried opened a few inches, and Gracie often got her fingers pinched. The magnets held the drawers closed, and seemed ideal. We installed them on the kitchen drawers and on Gracie's dresser drawers—she had, after all, started a game of getting up in the middle of the night and trying on everything in her drawers. I would wake up to find piles of clothes in the middle of the floor and all her socks lined up along the carpet in a bizarre sock parade.

Again, my little video recording device, also known as a toddler, was quick to learn the unlocking technique and discovered that all she had to do was retrieve the magnetic key. Every night we had to hide the key in out-of-reach places. The problem was that my husband was not as consistent as I was, and he would often place the key in his pocket and then leave the house for work. One morning I had to take Gracie to the store in her pajamas so I could buy more magnetic keys to open her dresser drawers. To be able to dress my daughter, I had to stash extra keys around the house. It became a game for Gracie to try to find them. My attempt at childproofing was becoming a competition, and my toddler was winning. Here again, childproofing was only managing to frustrate the adults.

Just as with the toilet locks, I realized I had dropped the ball in my parenting. Instead of locking things out of reach, I simply needed to be firm about what was and wasn't allowed. The locks came off the next morning.

Childproofing your home is important, but real childproofing comes from balancing how you set up your house with what you teach your children. My electrical outlets had covers when my kids were learning to crawl, but as soon as they were able to understand, we talked about what areas were not to be touched. Through this process, my kids learned that there were times when Mommy means business! Opening a dresser drawer to put on different pajamas would get you a raised eyebrow from Mommy, but pulling on a lamp cord would get you a finger waving, in-your-face confrontation, followed by a long stint in time-out. I liked this new method of childproofing. It was less frustrating for the adults and it was helping my kids learn that the world doesn't come with padded corners and soft places to land—unless, of course, you're talking about right here in Mommy's arms.

Jessica Is a Biter

By Kae

Jessica is a biter. I nursed her as a newborn, but had to stop after she got her first set of baby teeth. She would sometimes bite me so hard that she drew blood. (There's another item left out of my All the Goofy Advice About Babydom books.) When she started drinking from a bottle, I had to check the nipple after every feeding. She was notorious for chewing the nipples off.

One day, when she was about 14 months old, I went to get her up from her nap. When I leaned over to pick her up, I noticed that a huge hunk of the wood was missing from the end of the crib. Sure enough, there were scattered pieces of wood on the floor. At first I was confused. How could a huge hunk of solid oak just fall out onto the floor? Holding Jessica on my hip, I leaned in closer to look at the ragged hole where the wood used to be. To my amazement, there were tiny little teeth marks across the entire end of the crib. My child had gnawed a huge chunk out of a solid oak crib. I hadn't known she was part beaver.

You always had to be careful when Jessica's mouth was anywhere near your tender areas. As a baby, one of her favorite things was to snuggle her head into the crook of your neck. Then she would lovingly put her arms around your neck like you were about to get a great big hug. What you got instead was a wicked bite on the neck. How lucky was I? A hickey was my child's idea of loving interaction.

Christina was her main victim. By the time Jessica was two years old, any time she got angry, she would bite. When you have a child who is bright and stubborn and incapable of articulating her needs, you get a lot of angry moments. Poor Christina had been subjected to so many bites that I thought we should get her checked for rabies.

One day the girls were playing and I heard Christina begin to wail. I turned around to find her crying loudly and Jessica sitting next to her acting like nothing was happening.

"What's going on?" I asked as I walked over to where the girls were sitting. Frankly, when you are the mother of three, something is always "going on."

"She bit me." Christina held out her arm to show me a perfect imprint of Jessica's teeth.

I had done everything I knew to keep Jessica from biting. She had been spanked, had spent countless minutes in time-out, had been made to kiss the boo-boo and apologize to her sister, but nothing worked. She would say she was sorry one minute and have a hunk of Christina's flesh hanging from her jowls the next.

"You're going to have to bite her back," I said to the weeping Christina. I grabbed Jessica up by the same arm as the one that sported the angry red bite mark on Christina and offered it to Christina. "Bite her back so she'll know what it feels like. Maybe then she'll stop it."

"I can't bite her, it hurts," Christina said, as if my suggestion was the most ludicrous thing she had ever heard.

"You bite me, I don't care." Jessica stared her sister down, daring her to do it.

"I can't, it's not nice." Christina had begun to cry again. This was not the first time I realized that though Christina looks just like me, she is definitely genetically linked to her father. When I was a kid, if my mom gave me a free pass to take a shot at my brother, I would have been all in. David, on the other hand, was too soft-hearted to cause someone else distress, even if they deserved it. This was from whom my cute little blue-eyed blonde baby girl got her disposition. She was just too soft to do anything to distress Jessica. Looking between my two daughters, it came to me in a flash: If Christina looked just like me but had her daddy's temperament, then it made perfect sense that Jessica, who looked just like her daddy, would have mine.

Seeing the happy little glimmer in Jessica's eyes, I made a decision. "Fine," I said to Christina, "then I'll bite her for you." Still holding Jessica's arm in my hand, I pulled it up to my mouth and applied enough pressure with my teeth to make her eyes fly wide open. Jessica began to cry. She jumped into Christina's lap and sobbed, "I sorry, I sorry."

I know for a fact that I didn't bite the child hard enough to make her cry. I think she was just surprised to have someone give her a taste of her own medicine. I would like to tell you this was an epiphany for Jessica and that she never, ever bit her sister or any other unsuspecting human again. But that would be a lie. Basic instinct is hard to change. To this day, Jessica's first line of defense when she feels threatened is to bite. If she is ever accosted, we will be able to identify the perpetrator by the bite pattern somewhere on their body.

Big Girls Don't Cry

By Pam

Discipline is a difficult issue for mothers under the best of circumstances. Add the factor of being in public and you end up exhausting every last brain cell to find the right way to keep your family from being banned from the supermarket.

In public, you can't seem to ever win. If you spank your child in public, everyone around will look at you with scorn and disgust: Most of them will be ready to brand you as a child abuser. But if you don't spank your whining, tantrum-throwing child in public, you're still looked at with scorn and disgust because people are convinced you have absolutely no control.

Try getting down on your child's level and reasoning with him while in the middle of aisle seven and you'll get the looks of knowing empathy. Mothers before you have tried "the talk" many times while the ice cream is melting in the shopping cart. They know it has no effect. They smile at you and nod, as if offering silent, albeit useless, support. Then they steer their shopping carts as far away from you as possible.

Then there's the pathetic attempt at pretending to ignore the child who is turning red in the face and wailing in the middle of the cereal aisle. Yes, there are experts who say you should simply not give any attention to a tantrum-throwing child, but when you're in the middle of the supermarket or on the checkout line, people burn holes in you with their eyes. Regardless of how much you need the food in your shopping cart, you desperately want to abandon it, scoop up your precious little tear-stained siren, and run from the store, the parking lot, the neighborhood, the town, and perhaps the state.

Disciplining in private is no picnic either. Grandmothers, mothers, mothers-in-law, aunts, neighbors, friends, and even the cat seem to have opinions about what you're doing wrong. Like a sponge, you soak in all the advice you can in the hope that something someone says will work for you. You listen patiently to your best friend, nod respectfully at your mother-in-law, roll your eyes at your own mother, pretend you don't see the condescending looks from the cat, and continue to read the advice of authors who sound as if putting a child in time-out is the equivalent of a year in San Quentin. No matter how prepared you think you are when it comes to discipline, here's the reality: You're flying by the seat of your pants on this one. If you don't have gray hair yet, hang in there because there will be a bumper crop on your noggin any minute now.

As you struggle to find the best way to discipline your particular child, you will travel down a rocky road. Maybe, just maybe, you're one of the lucky ones who figures it all out immediately and is able to discipline your child without so much as a hair out of place. If you are that mom, you've earned the June Cleaver Award. If you can keep little Beaver in line without putting a wrinkle in your perfectly starched dress or having to bite on the pearl necklace around your neck, then more power to you. As for me? June Cleaver would've stripped me of my pearl necklace long ago.

As Kae will be the very first to tell you, I basically stink at discipline. Kae's children are well-behaved, they love her very much, their friends still tremble in her presence, but she's respected. Kae is a guard dog in Chihuahua's clothing. She is devoted, no-nonsense, and if you want to take the alpha dog title away from that petite woman, you'd better have good medical insurance. As for me, I'm basically a bunny rabbit who has moments of guard dog grandeur. A barking bunny rabbit—that perfectly describes my initial attempts at discipline when my children reached the age where they realized I wouldn't and couldn't actually bite.

Kae's approach to discipline has always been consistent and effective. You'd think that after knowing her for so many years, I would've picked up a few tips along the way. Nope. I had to figure it out for myself. That means trying one method after another and even then, my kids were so smart that whatever worked for the first three months might not work after that because they'd figured me out and knew how to manipulate the system. It's pretty sad when a three-year-old has you figured out, but let's be honest here—if intelligence were a prerequisite for motherhood, more than a few of us wouldn't make it.

So here's how the discipline road twisted and turned for me. Not being someone who wanted to spank my children, I first chose the time-out option. It seemed to make sense to me. When a child is acting up, the best option is not to give attention and to remove him or her from the situation. Sitting in one's room and contemplating one's navel seemed fairly reasonable. For many children, being sent to their toy-filled rooms is not a punishment. But—as I mentioned earlier—in our family attention was what was craved, so banishment to the bedroom was truly a trip to Siberia.

Time-outs seemed, for the most part, what were and still are effective in our house, but there have been times when they became a test of wills. Having ruled out the one minute for every year of age rule, I'd needed to find a more creative approach. But it wasn't always easy dealing with my clever kids.

"Jack," I said, kneeling beside my son after one apparently challenging situation, "do you know why I put you in time-out?"

"Yes," he muttered.

"Why are you in time-out?"

"Because you're a bad mommy."

"No, because you hit your sister, and hitting isn't nice."

"You're not nice!" Jack declared. "You're mean."

"Jack, you need to apologize to Gracie."

"You need to apologize to me!" he said as he folded his arms across his chest.

So Jack's time-out went into overtime.

Scott and I then tried to institute the time-out lasts as long as you're acting like a donkey's backside rule. The kids learned that they would sit in their rooms for as long as necessary until they regained control over their tempers and their manners. That worked, except when Gracie decided to take it as a challenge to stay in her room until we practically begged her to come out.

"Gracie," I said as I knelt down in front of her, "do you know why I put you in time-out?"

"Because I threw a toy at Jack," she replied.

I always felt hopeful at this point, because she always immediately acknowledged her crime without any venom. "Right. Now I want you to go apologize to Jack," I said.

"Later," she declared.

"Now," I said firmly.

"I'm staying in time-out."

"Why?" I asked.

"I like it here," she said and hunkered down into her time-out chair. There she would sit, and sit, and sit.

"Gracie," I said after she had spent quite a bit of time in her chair, "you've been in time-out for over an hour. Now go say you're sorry to Jack."

"I'm not ready."

My best method for dealing with her refusal to leave time-out was to leave her there and engage her brother in a fun (and loud) activity with the hope that Gracie's strong need to not miss out on family fun would get the best of her. Within a few moments, she'd appear in the hallway looking appropriately remorseful.

"I'm sorry, Jack."

Being the enlightened, modern mother that I am, I next tried the communication method. I figured my best approach would be to simply explain to my wonderful children why their behavior was unacceptable. As the enlightened, modern mother, I would find out the underlying cause for their behavior so I could help them through their frustration and offer an acceptable alternative. But being the enlightened, modern mother, I soon abandoned that approach when I quickly realized my kids didn't want to talk . . . they wanted to cry, sulk, scream, whine, point fingers, stomp their feet, and refuse to look at me.

Then one day I was watching TV and came upon the show Super Nanny. The fabulous TV nanny was using time-out mats, time-out chairs, and time-out beanbags. Maybe, I thought, I'm not using the correct time-out furniture. Perhaps an official time-out mat would do the trick. So off I went to the store and bought two large placemats to be used as our time-out mats. I explained the purpose of the mats to the children and they seemed to understand the seriousness of being made to sit on a placemat in the corner of the dining room. That is, until the first time-out occurred and the kids realized that the placemat on the hardwood floor was like a sled on snow. Back to the store I went for the time-out beanbag. That was too much fun to bounce on, so we tried a time-out chair. The time-out chair worked the best, but it still didn't address the issue of having to keep Jack in time-out far too long before he would stop fuming. And according to Super Nanny, you were supposed to request (and receive) an apology from your child at the end of time-out. Again, Gracie was up for the challenge and it became a matter of me forgetting about the apology or having Gracie stay in time-out until high school graduation.

Being a reasonably intelligent woman in other aspects of my life, I started to think I was coming at this from the wrong direction. When I'm doing a cat behavior consultation, I always tell my clients to focus on and reward the cat for any good behavior and not make a big deal about unwanted behavior. The cat, being a smart animal, will realize that it's more beneficial to behave acceptably. I realized I wasn't following my own advice. It was time to nip this discipline issue in the bud and stop being a barking bunny rabbit. I had an idea.

Off to the store I went for my supplies. That night, I called the kids into their rooms and showed them their new "star" charts. On each of their walls was a brightly colored chart with a list of good behaviors:

Make my bed
Dress myself
Eat my dinner
Put my dishes in the sink
Put my clothes in the hamper
Brush my teeth
Show respect/good manners
Show leadership
Listen to Mom and Dad
No time-outs
No answering back

Be nice to my brother/my sister
Show kindness to others
Put my toys away
Say my prayers

There were also some special things on the list based on whatever day of the week it was, such as showing respect at karate class or doing homework. I explained to Gracie and Jack what it meant to show leadership, ways to be kind to others, and how to make their beds (basically, just make sure the blanket lands on the bed and not the floor). At the end of each day, we would go over the chart; if a good behavior was displayed, a star would be placed there. Every time a child earned 30 stars, he or she would get a dollar to put in their brand new piggy banks. As the dollars mounted up in the bank, they would get divided into three envelopes—spending, saving, and giving. The kids could use the "spending" envelope to buy toys for themselves. The "saving" money was for big future purchases (Gracie has her eye on a convertible for her 16th birthday). The "giving" envelope would be for church tithes and charitable donations. I felt that if I were going to "pay" my children to be good, I would also teach them some valuable lessons about money.

I also explained that if they had a perfect day—a day where they earned stars for every behavior listed, they would get Mom's Special Stamp on their chart. This stamp declared GOOD JOB with a big smiley face. At that age, my kids valued stamps and stickers almost as much as toys.

The star chart continued to be the best learning tool for helping our children develop good manners and display good behavior. We adjusted the categories as the children aged and added bonus stars for extra-special behaviors. It also became a wonderful time for us to teach them all the ways they could show leadership, respect, and kindness.

I realize that some people may feel I resorted to bribery. But this method encouraged my children to be very honest about their accomplishments, learn from their setbacks, and feel appreciation for the toys they bought with their own money and their ability to make their own contributions toward the growth of our church. Our star chart even helped my children with their counting and reading skills. It wasn't a perfect system, but it emphasized all the good things my children did, and we all looked forward to seeing their progress on the star chart every night. We still had to include those old-fashioned time-outs, but for the most part, our star chart system brought peace to our home.

David in Time-Out

By Kae

On the subject of discipline, there are hundreds of theories. Some parents believe in spanking while others choose no corporal punishment. Some parents believe that children should be limited in TV viewing while others have TVs in their kids' rooms basically from birth. Some parents yell and others use their quiet, calm voices. Some parents say, "Because I said so." Others don't want to stifle their child's independence and attempt to reason with them instead. Some parents use time-out or the naughty chair, and others don't.

One concept of parenting that appeared to be unanimous in my All the Goofy Advice About Babydom reference collection was that parents should present a unified front when disciplining their children. The concept is great on paper. Unfortunately, David and I share an un-unified approach to discipline. We spent many years locked in the discipline wars.

My philosophy on discipline is simple: I am a mother, but I am also an individual. I have a basic personality that is humorously sarcastic and direct. As my husband is fond of telling me, I am as subtle as a sledgehammer. I have zero tolerance for bad children—or bad husbands for that matter. I am the alpha female in my household. I have earned my place at the top of the hierarchy of our family. I also firmly believe in my ability to determine the validity of my parental decisions. If I say to do—or not to do—something, it is "because I said so." and I expect it to be done or not done, whatever the case may be.

When my kids were young, I had a definite "take no prisoners" approach to discipline. A warning was always issued. If left unheeded, the punishment would commence. I was a strict parent. If a behavior was bad one day, it was bad every day. I did not turn a blind eye just to keep the family peace. I did not make excuses for my children's behavior. I expected them to behave under every circumstance. My approach was to address each breach in discipline as it unraveled and let the chips fall where they may.

In my defense, I was also a fun parent. I made sure the kids were fully aware that the only time I had to be "the mom" was when they forced my hand by not controlling their behavior. It was not a job I especially enjoyed; it was just a job I had agreed to do, and I planned to do it well.

David's parenting style was somewhat softer than mine. One thing that was then and still is immensely clear: he cannot stand it if a child is in distress. It doesn't matter to him if the child needs to be disciplined or not. All he knows is that the child is upset and he wants to make it better—immediately, no matter what the consequences. I have actually watched him openly glare at a strange woman in a department store because she was disciplining her child, even though he had no idea what the child had done to be receiving the discipline.

Matthew was the first of our children to exploit his father's softness. He would covertly poke or prod me, intentionally doing something that he knew for a fact was going to get him in trouble. Sure enough, as soon as I'd had enough and was taking off after him, he would go running down the hall yelling, "Daddy! Daddy!" at the top of his lungs. David would come around the corner right on cue. Now it was time to see which David was coming and to whose rescue. Sometimes I got the supportive husband who banded with me as a parental unit, and we disciplined the child together. Other times I got the "don't distress my child" David. It was this David who sparked some of the Allen family's best arguments.

"Don't yell at Matthew!"

Ugh, it's the "don't distress my child" David.

"How do you know what he's doing? You weren't even in the room."

"It doesn't matter, you don't have to yell."

And so the standard argument would ensue. The "don't distress my child" David was indignant at the notion that his child was being yelled at or sent to time-out or, heaven forbid, spanked.

I was hell bent on handing out the punishment I had warned the child was coming if the behavior didn't stop.

When the "don't distress my child" David was in attendance, Matthew was thrilled. He had figured out a way to get me into trouble, and he was overjoyed. For the next several days, Matthew's behavior would be out of control. He talked back, poked, and pushed my buttons so that I would lose my temper. Each time, the "don't distress my child" David came to his rescue and the standard argument started up.

One evening David was in his home office and I was in the bathroom helping the kids get ready for bed. All three children had had their baths and were brushing their teeth. Matthew was the last one done with his teeth. Just as he was finishing up, he turned and spit on me. That was it. The final straw. "Matthew, I am going to spank your butt," I said as he ran out of the bathroom and headed down the hallway screaming, "Daddy, Daddy, she's going to hit me!"

Like Matthew's knight in shining armor, the "don't distress my child" David came rushing out of the office doorway. He was like a raging bull; there was no way I was going to spank one of his children. He didn't care about Matthew's behavior. Matthew was rescued. As they walked down the hallway toward Matthew's bedroom, the kid turned around and gave me a sly little smile. He had won the fight.

Later that evening when the stories were read and we were tucking the children into their beds, I told Matthew how disappointed I was in his behavior. "From now on, I am not going to yell at you or spank you when your daddy is here. That way I don't have to argue with Daddy because it hurts my feelings. I know you are doing this on purpose to get your daddy and me into fights." Matthew smiled a little smile with a gleam in his eye. In his five-year-old mind, he had figured out a way to do anything he wanted and not get into trouble.

"What I am going to do is keep score. I am going to mark down every time you should be in trouble. Your daddy can't stay home forever. The next time he leaves the house, I am going to bust your butt. So you just go ahead and act any way you want to." I kissed him on the forehead and wished him a good night.

Matthew failed to heed the warning. For the next several days his behavior was deplorable. He picked at his sister; he picked at me. I refused to rise to the bait; I just made a mental note, biding my time.

Sure enough, several days later David had to go to the copy shop to have some documents printed. I watched the car pull out of our driveway and turn right at the corner. I left the window and went to our family room where Matthew was playing nicely with his Hot Wheels. I walked in and, without saying a word, applied a moderate amount of psychology to his rear end. "Your daddy can't stay home all the time," I reminded him as I left the room.

It was a miracle. Matthew was cured. After that day, he stopped, for the most part, intentionally trying to get David and me into fights.

No matter how many times David took the children's side when they were being punished, it never failed to amaze me that an adult would take the side of a child in an argument with another adult. Especially not when the other adult is his wife, the woman he trusts in all aspects of his life—as long as it doesn't cause his children distress.

All parents have to develop a discipline style they can live with. Whenever David was forced to discipline a child, he would spend the next several hours feeling guilty and upset. I have never understood this feeling. I must have been born with that gene missing. I disciplined my children because it was my job. I have never felt bad about applying psychology to their backsides, sending them to the edge of the bed, or just torturing them in their teenage years with the dreaded "talks" about their behavior.

The day I decided to bring the children into my life, I entered into an unwritten contract with them. I promised to do my best to make sure they grew up to be the best, most well-adjusted, productive members of society they could be. As my children grew out of the baby stage and into their adolescent years, I made a deal with them: They were going to be raised the way I thought was best, whether they agreed or not. If I screwed them up, I would pay for their therapy.

Nothing angered me more than not having David support me when it came to disciplining the children. And quite honestly, it hurt my feelings because I assumed he took the children's side because he felt like I was a bad parent. The reality was, he took their side because he literally could not stand to see them distressed in any way.

The worst battle in the David vs. Kae discipline wars was the day I found David in Matthew's room after Matthew had been sent to time-out. I knew something was up because I saw David sneaking out of our back hall. I looked in the doorway just in time to see David slipping Matthew a cookie!

I was livid. "How dare you give Matthew a cookie when he's in time-out?" I snatched the cookie from Matthew's hand. "Are you completely out of your mind? Have you gone insane? It's bad enough I have to be the bad guy, but now you're giving him cookies when he's in trouble."

David and Matthew sat stock still on the side of the bed with eyes as big as saucers. They both knew there was no way they were getting out of this one.

"You're the one that sent him away from the dinner table before he was done," David countered, "so, I thought, you know, that he might be hungry. He's a growing boy."

"You know what, if you want to act like one of the children, then fine. You can just sit right here in time-out with Matthew. Both of you put your hands in your laps and hang your heads in shame. Don't either one of you dare move until you can apologize for what you've done."

David stood up and started to say something. Gauging the look on my face, he decided that sitting back down and being quiet might be a better option.

I took the cookie to the kitchen and pitched it into the garbage pail. I peeked back in the room to make sure David didn't bring milk to go with the cookie. Fortunately for both my little men, they sat, side by side, hands folded in their laps, heads hung in shame. I would never have thought that as a mother, I would have to put my husband in time-out. But there he was, a full-grown man with a law degree from Northwestern University, looking like the mirror image of his five-year-old son who hadn't yet graduated from kindergarten.

A few minutes later, I heard a chorus of "Mommy" and "Kae" coming from Matthew's room. I went to Matthew's bedroom door and said, "Did you two learn anything you want to tell me about?"

They both nodded their heads in unison.

"Matthew, what did you learn?"

"Not to take cookies from Daddy?"

"And what else?"

"Not to play with Steenie's food."

"David, what did you learn?"

"Not to give Matthew cookies."

"How about we just don't give Matthew cookies when he's in time-out."

"Okay."

Both my little men got up from the edge of the bed, gave me hugs, and apologized again for their behavior.

That night, after the children had gone to bed, David and I had a long talk about how it wasn't good for the children for him to act the way he did when they got into trouble. He agreed with all his heart. He promised he would never intentionally make me out to be the bad guy with the kids. But each time one of the children misbehaved and an altercation between mother and child ensued, it was always a crapshoot as to which David would be there. Quite often, I got the "don't distress my child" David. But I was sometimes pleasantly surprised to get the supportive husband I've grown to know and love.

I guess I could have given up on the discipline my children needed. I guess I could have killed David and buried him in our dirt-floor basement. Both options seemed irresponsible.

For many years while the children were growing up, David and I made jokes (sometimes in humor, sometimes not so much) about how we would never fight again after the children were raised and out of the house. It's turned out to be true. Our children have been grown and moved out of our house for years now, and David and I rarely argue. I think this is because I have developed the ability to just look at him and say, "Really, you're taking the dog's side?"

Chapter 3

A Mess a Day . . .

Speed Painting

By Pam

Scott was out of town for the weekend at a seminar. It was also the weekend my in-laws invited the extended family to dinner to check out a new restaurant that had just opened in town. That meant I had to handle my two-year-old and four-year-old on my own in a public dining situation. Normally, that wouldn't have worried me too much. But with my in-laws in the same public dining situation, there was cause to worry. Rumor had it that my parenting skills were not in line with the way things were done "in the old days," and without Scott as my buffer, there was plenty of opportunity for me to be cornered like the weak zebra in the herd, about to be brought down by the lions.

I bathed the kids and got them dressed in outfits given to them by their grandma. Okay, I'm not above trying to score brownie points and I had to use whatever ammunition I could. All that was left was for me to get dressed. That meant my kids needed to remain occupied and clean for about 15 minutes. I popped a movie into the DVD player and headed to my bedroom.

I had just about finished dressing and was putting on my shoes when I heard my children laughing. To me, the sweetest sound in the world is the sound of a child's laughter. The innocent giggling of a child watching something funny or being gently ticked is medicine for my heart. As sweet as that laughter can be, though, there is also a type of childish laughter that sends chills down a mother's spine. That's when the innocent crosses over into mischievous. That bad, cackling laughter usually means the child is finding thrills in doing something forbidden, such as drawing a permanent marker mustache on a sibling's favorite doll or flushing the car keys down the toilet. That was the kind of laughter I heard as I dropped my shoe and ran into the sunroom where my kids were supposed to be watching the DVD. They weren't there. Crap! I heard the evil giggling behind me. It was coming from the playroom. As I headed in that direction, I saw my car keys on the counter. At least I knew they hadn't taken that fatal swim into the septic tank.

I turned and ran with one shoe on into the playroom. Standing in the doorway, I had to close my eyes for a moment because I was sure I was dreaming. In the few minutes I had been dressing in the bedroom, Gracie had managed to reach the paint set on the top shelf of the closet (a height only a monkey could climb, so how she did it remains a mystery to me), and she and Jack had started painting. The two pieces of paper with a few splotches of paint on them lay ignored on the play table. The majority of the paint was on my children. What must've started out as an attempt at finger painting had apparently turned into total body art. Their outfits from grandma were polka-dotted with multicolored paint. Gracie is normally a very meticulous child and hates getting even the smallest amount of dirt on her clothes. I was always telling her to loosen up and enjoy the childhood fun of getting dirty. But why did she choose that moment to finally follow my advice?

How they managed to get that much paint on them in such a short time amazed me. I looked at my watch. It was getting late, so I had no time to wonder about my children's newfound talent for speed painting. I carefully stripped off their clothes and carried each one at arm's length into the bathroom. They were about to get their second bath in less than one hour to remove the paint from their arms, hair, and other body parts.

I stood Jack in the tub and hosed him down with warm water, threw a towel around him and then sent him off to his room. Gracie was next. As I started rinsing her hair I saw the water in the tub turn purple. I looked down at my tan shirt and sure enough, there were purple spots of paint across my chest.

When the fast baths were complete, I yanked the hair dryer out of the drawer and proceeded to dry Gracie's hair. After her first bath that day, I had taken the time to carefully dry her beautiful, thick hair into soft waves. This time around I was only concerned with removing most of the water so she wouldn't freeze when we went outside into the late winter air.

Once dried, I herded my confused and complaining children (two baths in one hour brings out the worst in a child) into their bedrooms to get dressed. I looked at the clock. We were now 20 minutes late. There was no time to lose.

Five minutes later we were out the door and headed toward the restaurant. Luckily, my in-laws tended to run late, so my delay probably wouldn't be noticed.

We arrived at the restaurant just as my in-laws were walking in the door. I quickly got Gracie and Jack out of their cat seats and dashed toward the restaurant. Just before going inside, I took a deep breath, straightened my shirt, and looked down at myself. I had forgotten to change my shirt. I buttoned my jacket to hide the purple spots.

I bent down to talk to my children and reminded them that they were to be on their best behavior. It was then that I noticed Gracie had one bright red eyebrow and Jack had green paint in his ear. I refused to be the weak zebra in the herd. I still had time to fix this.

We walked into the restaurant and quickly greeted everyone. I casually kept one hand over Jack's ear and the other on Gracie's head so no one would notice the paint.

"Excuse us for a moment," I said to everyone, "I'm just going to quickly take them to the restroom before we sit down."

"But Mommy," Gracie started to say, "we already went . . ." Before she could finish, I spun them around and headed toward the bathroom.

A wet paper towel removed their red and green paint. Before leaving the bathroom, I did a quick once-over to make sure I hadn't missed any other spots. Other than Gracie's straggly-looking hair from the quick blow-drying, my children looked good. We could now sit down to a wonderful dinner.

Back at the table, things were going well. My children were on their best behavior. After the speed-painting incident, I didn't have any time to properly reprimand them, so on the drive over I told them that if they behaved perfectly throughout dinner, they would escape punishment. The kids thought that was a great deal. They impressed everyone at the table with their impeccable manners. I was starting to relax and actually enjoy myself.

But the restaurant was very warm, and while engaged in conversation with one of my sisters-in-law, I absentmindedly removed my jacket.

"What happened to your shirt?" my sister-in-law gasped. Everyone turned to look.

The doomed zebra stood on the African plain, and watched the lions begin to circle around her.

Hey, That's My Diploma

By Kae

In 1985, I went back to college. I began my renewed college career juggling the demands of being a full-time mother to 15-month-old Matthew and a full-time wife to David. In 1986, I gave birth to my second child, Christina. I stopped going to school during the day and took a full class load at night. My days were consumed with taking care of two children and keeping up a house. At night I shifted gears and became an accounting student. In 1989, my third child was born. That same year, David and I moved to Tennessee to start our life as entrepreneurs.

I spent the next 18 months taking one class each semester at night, while being a full-time mother to three children and secretary to David's new law practice. I also began working for a court reporter, typing transcripts to make a few extra dollars, and started my own business as a bookkeeper for local businesses.

When we moved to Tennessee, I had three classes left to finish my degree. I finished my last class in May of 1991 at Middle Tennessee State University, and then transferred the credits back to Elmhurst College in Illinois, my former school, so I could graduate.

I assumed that because it was a long drive to Chicago, we wouldn't bother to attend graduation at Elmhurst; I would just get my diploma in the mail. David, however, was having none of that. He insisted we make the trip. Friday afternoon, after Matthew got out of school, we packed up our trusty blue Ford Taurus station wagon and made the nine-hour trip back to Western Springs, Illinois, to stay with my in-laws so we could attend the ceremony on Saturday.

Graduation Day, David woke me up and told me to get ready because he was taking me out for breakfast to celebrate. My mother- and father-in-law were going to get the kids ready and bring them later. I was shocked to find out that not only were my in-laws coming, but my sister-in-law and brother-in-law would also be there with their little boy.

David made me feel like the queen of the universe that day. He doted on me, got my cap on straight, and took all kinds of pictures. He told me many times that he was proud of me.

My mother-in-law said that as each of our children was born, she and my father-in-law discussed the likelihood that I would not finish school. When we moved to Tennessee, it was a done deal in their minds—I would never finish. She told me she was surprised and proud that I had reached my goal.

As the ceremony began, I walked in a line with the other graduates and took my seat. I listened attentively as the speakers gave their inspirational speeches on the subject of beginning our adult lives. In truth, I kind of snickered to myself at this.

My adult life had begun eight years ago. Finally, it was time to receive our diplomas. Until this moment, despite all the support I'd been receiving, the monumental accomplishment that the day represented had not dawned on me. But as I stood in the line, inching forward with each name called, the memories of the last six years flashed through my mind: the hours I'd spent rocking a child in a Kanga-Rocka-Roo while doing homework; the hours in the backyard while the kids played and I sat on a blanket reading a textbook; the mad rushes back and forth to the college so I wouldn't have to pay extra on the daycare bill; the number of nights I walked home from college in the dark after my night classes let out, jumping at the sound of every leaf that blew down the sidewalk.

All of a sudden, everything I had done out of necessity, not giving it a second thought at the time, came flashing into my mind. My mother-in-law was right. It was a miracle that I was here today. When I walked across the stage when my name was called, my family erupted into applause. I realized I was also proud of myself. There had been so many reasons to quit. So many times when giving up the dream of finishing college to fall into the role of housewife and mother would have been the path of least resistance.

After the ceremony was over, my family greeted me with hugs and congratulations. My children didn't really understand what was going on, but they knew it was something special because the man on the stage called their mommy's name. David was snapping pictures of me with the kids. My mother-in-law has a picture of herself with both her kids at graduation wearing their graduation caps—I was honored that she wanted David to take a similar picture of herself with me. During the picture taking, Jessica wanted me to hold her. I picked her up and held her on one hip while we finished taking pictures. At one point I looked down and there was my daughter with my diploma stuck in her mouth.

I guess some mothers would have grabbed the diploma from the kid's mouth and wiped the spit off the corner before it stained. To me, it seemed completely appropriate that the diploma I had sacrificed and strove for was branded forever in the upper-left-hand corner with my child's slobber.

Glow in the Dark

By Pam

When your child is a baby, you have total control over the toothbrush and toothpaste selection. You may not, however, have total control over whether that toothbrush will get past the steel jaws of the child. When a baby doesn't want to open his mouth, nothing short of the jack from a car will pry those lips open. Luckily, tooth brushing was relatively easy when Jack and Gracie were babies. My trouble started when they became older and developed specific toothbrush preferences.

I learned two lessons very quickly about toothbrush selection. Lesson one: Never take the kids when shopping for toothbrushes. Going down the dental hygiene aisle was like going down the candy aisle. Winnie the Pooh, Dora the Explorer, Spider-Man, and every other cartoon character beckoned my children to bring them home. Lesson two: Always buy the same toothbrush for both kids. You might think my girly-girl of a daughter would've preferred Cinderella over Batman, but if Jack wanted Batman, Gracie wanted Batman. If Gracie wanted Barbie, Jack wanted Barbie.

The toothbrush obsession didn't start right away. Initially, my children were blissfully happy with their ordinary brushes with no characters at all. Since Mommy or Daddy were the ones doing the brushing, the children didn't even see much of the toothbrushes. They just opened their mouths and then obediently spit in the sink when instructed. Then, the second that tooth brushing time was over, they shot out of the bathroom as fast as they could.

I was responsible for our toothbrush debacle. The day I innocently introduced character toothbrushes into the household in an effort to entice my kids into brushing longer, the downward spiral began. Gracie and Jack became watchful of each other and would race into the bathroom to snag the brush they knew the other one wanted.

"Gracie, why are you using Jack's Spider-Man brush?" I asked.

"Because it was in my toothbrush holder," she declared.

"How did it get in your toothbrush holder?" I asked.

No answer.

"Gracie, how did Jack's toothbrush get in your toothbrush holder?" I asked firmly.

"It jumped in there," she declared triumphantly.

No surprise; inanimate objects in our home had a knack for unexpectedly switching locations without any toddler assistance.

I quickly learned that the best way to handle this was to buy the same toothbrush for each child whenever it was time to replace the brushes.

A few months later, Jack discovered his toddler masculinity and declared that he would no longer use any toothbrush containing "girly" colors and became adamant about not having anything pink, purple, or sparkly on his side of the bathroom counter. Gracie was fine with boy-themed toothbrushes but Jack had turned a testosterone corner. Girl stuff was yucky.

Our next few months we bought only Spider-Man, Batman, and any other boy's toothbrush we could find. Gracie was happy and Jack was happy. That happiness didn't last long, though.

You would think I'd have left well enough alone, but no, I had to mess up a good thing. I received coupons in the mail for a "buy one get one free" battery-operated toothbrush for children. Never being one to pass up a good deal, I bought two of these toothbrushes on the next trip to the supermarket. I wasn't totally stupid, though, because I bought two Scooby-Doo brushes and passed up the cute little Cinderella brush.

The kids loved the brushes and it helped extend their brushing time—something I liked because it meant they'd do a better job at cleaning. If only one toothbrush hadn't broken a few weeks into my plan, life would've been good. But when Jack's toothbrush broke and he had to watch Gracie use her electric one while he was back in the Stone Age with his old manual one, tooth brushing time turned into sulking time.

Musical toothbrushes were the next items I brought home. The theory behind these brushes is that the children are supposed to brush until the music stops. They broke as well.

My worst toothbrush purchase was the glow-in-the-dark brush. You push down on the end of the brush and it flashes bright red for two minutes—adequate brushing time. The kids loved them. We turned out the bathroom light, and my kids looked in the mirror at their alien-like faces with glowing mouths. They would brush the entire two minutes and would've gladly brushed another two. I thought I had finally hit a dental hygiene home run.

We stopped using the glow-in-the-dark toothbrushes when I discovered my kids were sneaking into the bathroom at night, retrieving their toothbrushes, and using them as flashlights under the covers in bed, under the bed, in their underwear, and in the closet. They would put the toothbrushes in their shoes to watch their sneakers light up. With my germophobia, those toothbrushes were not going anywhere near their mouths after having been in contact with underwear and shoes.

We are now back to using boring, ordinary toothbrushes. There are no characters on them. They do not play a tune. They do not vibrate. They do not swivel. They do not have sonic waves that blast food from the teeth. They do not light up. They do nothing but have white bristles on them. They are as generic as toothbrushes get. Although, I did happen to see this cool fluorescent flossing tool my kids might like . . .

I'll never learn.

Band-Aids

By Kae

There must be a covert organization that targets children for the Band-Aid industry—the Committee for the Promotion of Band-Aid Revenue or something like that. Before my children could talk, a box of Band-Aids would sit for years languishing on the medicine cabinet shelf, sandwiched between a half-empty bottle of alcohol and a brown bottle of hydrogen peroxide.

To tell the truth, I have never been much on keeping up a proper medicine cabinet. In fact, we don't have an actual medicine cabinet. If you get a cough or need some cold medicine, you go to the drugstore. Drugstores are amazing places if you're sick. There are aisles and aisles of remedies for what ails you. I never understood the concept of attempting to guess what ailment was going to befall me so I could stock up on the necessary remedies in advance. If I am too sick to go to the drugstore, I should probably bypass that stop and go directly to the doctor's office or the emergency room.

The first time I stocked up on anything medicinal was when Matthew started walking. His knees stayed bruised and bloody from falls on our concrete driveway, so I kept a tube of antibacterial ointment and a box of Band-Aids in the kitchen at all times. His knees got so bad I sewed padding in the knees of some of his long sweatpants to cushion the blows. I also tried to make sure his scratched-up knees stayed slathered with ointment and covered with Band-Aids at all times. I am almost certain this is where the boo-boo-Band-Aid connection was forged.

Seven years and two more children later, I was spending a small fortune on Band-Aids. It seemed as if every time I turned around, one of the kids was crying and pointing to a boo-boo (some visible to the naked eye, some not) that needed a Band-Aid on it to make it stop hurting. Since I was unaware of the Committee for the Promotion of Band-Aid Revenue at that time, I unwittingly continued to purchase Band-Aids with abandon.

One day I used the last Band-Aid in the box. When the next child appeared with a boo-boo, she was told the Band-Aid box was empty. The boo-boo was treated with a magic kiss and off she was sent. Word spread like wildfire among the children that the Band-Aid box was empty. For each new boo-boo, the magic kiss was administered and off the injured party went. Over the next several days, it became apparent that there was a direct correlation between the number of boo-boos my children had and the number of Band-Aids available to apply to said boo-boos: No Band-Aids, no boo-boos. Once I was sure of the boo-boo–Band-Aid correlation, I refused to buy a new supply of Band-Aids. And when the kids realized there were no more Band-Aids and that none were going to be purchased any time soon, they miraculously stopped needing them.

To my amazement, my children, who I was positive had all been born with the dreaded double klutz gene, were suddenly less accident-prone. Tumbles were taken and the children were picking themselves up, dusting themselves off, and moving on to the next adventure, free from the sticky application of a Band-Aid.

Now, I am not going to suggest they led a boo-boo-free existence. Very few children escape the first five years of life without at least one black eye administered by the edge of a coffee table. And anyone who has raised a child knows that children's knees and elbows are prone to big, bloody scrapes. The shin of every child under the age of five is marred with the healing scars from a fall off the swing set or a tumble down the back steps. So every once in a while a boo-boo would require some sort of dressing to keep the child's blood off my sofa. In these instances, a folded piece of toilet paper or paper towel held in place with a strip of Scotch tape did the trick.

For my children, Band-Aids became an exciting extravagance. They were so scarce in our house that they began making their way into the children's Christmas stockings. The kids were very excited when they pulled out the brightly colored box of Band-Aids with cartoon characters on them. They paraded around the house sporting their Batman or Cabbage Patch Kids Band-Aids on their multitude of boo-boos. By the end of January, though, things in the Allen house would be back to normal. With all the Christmas Band-Aids used up, the number of boo-boos diminished drastically.

When Pam's husband, Scott, was at our house doing some major remodeling, he cut his finger one day and began to bleed. Christina said, "Wait, I'll get you a Band-Aid," and, to Scott's surprise, handed him a folded piece of paper towel and some Scotch tape.

When Matt was about 27, we were reupholstering the seats in his truck when he cut his finger on my new scissors. He uttered an expletive and rushed into the bathroom. To my amusement, he washed out the cut and held a wad of toilet paper against it. He then picked up the duct tape we were working with and wrapped it liberally around his finger. He held his finger up to me. "See Mom, all better."

On a Roll

By Pam

Paper towels are the safe barrier between all things yucky and me. A giant wad of paper towels is the only way I can kill any unfortunate bug that finds itself in my home. I'm sure many of the ones I've managed to grasp with my pillow of paper towels didn't even die, but rather just lounged in the softness as I carried them to the trash can. Looking back, I'm beginning to think my first apartment in New York wasn't as infested with roaches as I had thought—perhaps it was simply the same roach being captured, put in the trash, escaping, and being recaptured by me.

When I first adopted cats, my paper towel use increased considerably. When you're a germophobe, you can be lulled into a false sense of security by the sparkling white disguise the towel offers as it covers whatever gross liquid has been expelled from your pets. No matter how little money I had or how much I needed to budget every expense, a big wad of papers towels was a necessity when it came to picking up a hairball or wayward kitty poop.

Yes, I confess, I have been a paper towel over-user since I can remember, and motherhood has only fueled that excessive consumption. There's probably a landfill somewhere piled high with my mountains of used paper towels. I have tried to make up for it in other ways, by recycling and using cloth shopping bags and earth-friendly cleaning products, but the truth is, I've never met a paper towel I didn't want to use.

My love and overuse of paper towels came face-to-face with harsh reality when I became a mother. It began on an afternoon when I was not feeling well and was taking a nap on the couch in my sunroom. My children were being especially cooperative and were busy doing a puzzle in the dining room. It was too good to be true; mothers aren't supposed to be able to nap when they're feeling sick. I should have known something bad was about to happen.

After napping for almost an hour, I woke up realizing that whatever illness I had was more serious than I'd thought. I was chilled to the bone, but my skin was burning up. I dragged myself up from the couch to head to the bathroom for aspirin and a temperature check. My sunroom is separated from the dining room by a set of French doors. As I got closer to the doors, I saw something very odd. The floor and much of the furniture in my dining room seemed to be covered in something white. I'd left my eyeglasses on the table by the couch, so I couldn't be totally sure, but it looked like snow. It couldn't be, I said to myself. I looked through the French doors again. Yes, it was certainly extremely white in the dining room. I figured my fever must've been higher than I thought and that I now was hallucinating.

I stumbled back to the couch, snatched my glasses off the end table, and went back toward the dining room. I looked through the French doors again, and sure enough, it was white everywhere. This wasn't a good sign. My head was throbbing, I had a fever, and I knew that whatever was happening in the dining room wasn't going to contribute to my recovery. As I opened the door, I saw my kids grinning at me from behind mountains of white. I quickly closed the door and backed away. I evaluated the situation: sick mom, strange white stuff taking over my dining room, and two grinning kids. I felt too sick, and therefore too short-tempered, to handle whatever bizarre event was taking place in my formerly clean dining room. I headed for the garage, where my husband was working on a project.

"Strange . . . white stuff . . . snow . . . dining room . . . kids . . . I'm sick . . . dining room . . . kids . . . white stuff . . . fever," I rattled off as I stood in the doorway.

Scott took one look at me, felt my forehead, and declared that I was burning up and must be hallucinating. He said he'd go check on the kids. I slowly followed.

Before I could reach the French doors leading to the dining room, Scott quickly came back toward me. "Stay in the sunroom," he said, directing me away from the door, "Lie on the couch. Don't go into the dining room."

"What did they do?" I asked, worried. Maybe there really was snow in there.

"You don't want to know," he replied, "I'll take care of it. Promise me you won't look."

"Oh, God, what have they done?"

"It's not that bad, but you'll freak out," Scott said.

My husband knows me very well. He has lovingly accepted that he married a germophobe with OCD. He has resigned himself to the fact that if he puts a half-filled glass of juice down on a table I will probably pick it up, empty the juice in the sink, and put the glass in the dishwasher whether he has finished with it or not. He knows I have a very itchy trigger finger when it comes to a can of Lysol. He's used to my talent of being able to catch a falling food crumb from across the room before it hits the floor. He knows my quirks and has resigned himself to them. I'm a very fortunate woman.

I headed back to the couch and tried to go back to sleep. Through my fever fog I heard lots of scurrying back and forth coming from the other side of the French doors. Since I hadn't seen Scott return to the garage to retrieve our snow shovel, I felt confident that it wasn't snow that covered my hardwood floors.

After about half an hour, I looked up and my two children were standing before me, appearing rather sheepish, with my husband behind them. The kids were no longer grinning.

"Okay," he said to Gracie and Jack, "tell Mommy you're sorry."

"We're sorry, Mommy," they said in unison.

"What did you do?" I asked.

"We spilled some juice," Gracie replied.

"And?" Scott prodded her.

"We used too many paper towels to clean it up," she admitted.

My kids wanted juice, but they didn't want to disturb me. So Gracie, being the big sister, decided she would get the refreshments herself. Attempting to put eight ounces of juice into a six-ounce cup, she ended up spilling some on the counter. While cleaning up the juice on the counter, she knocked the already filled cup onto the floor. Not wanting to awaken me (or get themselves in trouble), both kids grabbed paper towels to mop up the floor.

Not being experienced in calculating the amount of paper towels needed to absorb a juice spill, and apparently also feeling an overwhelming need to turn clean-up into fun since Mommy was asleep in the other room, my kids decided more was better. When they used up all the paper towels on one roll, they headed to the closet for a new one. This was repeated more than a dozen times.

If you're curious about how many paper towels it takes to completely engulf the average dining room in white, making it look as if three feet of snow has fallen, the answer is 1,218—two-ply at that! That's 14 rolls of paper towels used that day to clean up about eight ounces of liquid.

As punishment, both children had to fork over money from their piggy banks to pay for the 1,218 paper towels. That night during bedtime prayers, Jack also apologized to God for "wasting however many trees it takes to make 14 rolls of paper towels."

Chapter 4

Panic Early, Panic Often

Daddy, That's My Gum

By Kae

David eventually gave up his "sugar is the root of all evil" approach to parenting and allowed the children to have candy in severely limited quantities. On top of our refrigerator was an antique enamel cooking pot that was the designated candy bowl. Anytime the children were given sugary morsels, they were required to put them in the candy bowl. David would then dispense the treats in what he considered was an appropriate manner.

Candy was therefore a prime commodity in our house, and gum was almost unheard of. That was my idea. I had an intense dislike for hearing anyone chewing with an open mouth. If the sound of someone smacking a juicy mouthful is a major irritant, the last thing you want to do is give your child a piece of gum, thereby providing an open-ended chewing experience.

"Mommy, look what I got," Christina said as she rushed into my home office one day after school. She held her prize reverently in her chubby little five-year-old hands. She looked up at me with her bright blue eyes and slowly opened her hands like a flower blooming. There, sitting in her palms, was a bright yellow stick of Juicy Fruit gum.

"Very nice," I said, inspecting her prize with the proper amount of reverence. "Let's put it in the kitchen. Maybe you can have it after dinner," I added as we headed down the hallway. Just then the office telephone rang and I sprinted back down the hall to answer it before the machine picked up. Christina, left on her own, made the right decision. Instead of heading off into her bedroom and hiding the piece of gum in her underwear drawer, she continued down the hallway toward the kitchen. Just as I had asked, she laid her prize stick of Juicy Fruit on the kitchen counter and went off to find Matthew and Jessica.

Later that afternoon, David and I were standing in the kitchen deep in discussion. David was leaning up against the counter when Christina came in. Christina loved to be in the same room with us. Today she was hanging out in the kitchen listening to David and me discuss some mundane issue of securities law. David spied the piece of gum on the counter and picked it up. This definitely got Christina's attention. She walked over to David as he began fooling with the bright yellow wrapper.

My husband has a unique skill I have never quite figured out how to master: selective hearing. "Daddy, that's my gum," Christina said as she stood directly in front of him, tipping her head back to look him in the face.

David kept talking, intent on making his point. He absent-mindedly continued to unwrap the gum.

"Daddy, that's my gum," Christina said again, a bit more frantic this time. She was beginning to bounce on her toes directly in front of David, still with her head tipped back.

There was no indication that David realized Christina was there. He pulled the bright yellow wrapper off the stick of gum and began working on the silver packaging.

"Daddy, that's my gum," Christina said with real panic in her voice. Now she was bouncing up and down in front of David like a rabid kangaroo, desperate to get his attention.

Still, David never heard a word. Deep in discussion, he pulled the silver wrapper off the stick of gum.

"Daddy, that's my gum," Christina's voice had raised another octave on the panic chart.

David nonchalantly folded the stick of gum in half.

"Daddy, that's my gum." At this point, Christina had taken up this phrase as a rapid chant, rising in pitch with each repetition. She was jumping wildly up and down, clawing at the front of David's pants in a last-ditch effort to get his attention.

"Daddy, that's my gum. Daddy, that's my gum. Daddy, that's my gum."

Finally, without a second thought, David popped the coveted piece of Juicy Fruit into his mouth. Christina let out one last banshee wail of "Daddy, that's my gum!" Seeing her precious piece of gum disappear into David's mouth, she crumpled to the floor in tears.

Finally, David noticed Christina. He looked down at the puddle on the floor that represented his precious five-year-old daughter. With the quizzical look of someone who has just woken up in the middle of a class with everyone staring at them, he asked, "What?"

Luckily for David, we live about one block away from a small grocery store. With his red-eyed, sniffling five-year-old in tow, David headed out the front door to buy Christina not just one piece of Juicy Fruit but an entire package.

Hide and Seek

By Pam

One aspect of my personality that I used to think of as a good quality is that I don't wait until the last minute to get things done. I have a need to get on with a task and finish it. I hate to have unfinished projects hanging over my head. I also like to do things myself, and I don't like waiting around for other people. This has been a benefit for my husband when Christmas Eve rolls around. While many husbands are up until the wee hours of the morning playing Santa and assembling toys, Scott can get his eight hours of sleep; I have already fully assembled everything.

I don't do this out of some unselfish love for my husband. I do this because of some quirk in my personality that requires me to have the presents bought, assembled, wrapped, and hidden in the attic at least two weeks before Christmas. The only reasons I can think of for this behavior are that I'm obsessive-compulsive and that I'm a writer and regularly live with deadlines. Maybe there's also some other deep, dark reason why I must get everything bought, wrapped, and hidden so far in advance, but discovering it would probably involve therapy.

Christmas Eve 2006, the kids were fed, bathed, and in their pajamas. We bundled up, got in the car, and drove through the neighborhood to look at the holiday lights. Afterward, we came home and watched a DVD of Rudolph the Red-Nosed Reindeer. Right before bed, we bundled up again and went out onto the front lawn to spread our special reindeer food. Then it was back inside to set out a plate of milk and cookies for Santa. Once tucked into bed, the kids were read the classic The Night Before Christmas, and then lights were out.

As I walked out of Gracie's room after kissing her goodnight, I heard her call across the hall to Jack: "Hey, Jack, do you know what Santa does with the stockings on the fireplace?"

"No," answered her sleepy brother.

"He fills them full of candy and little toys," she said.

"Really?" asked Jack, who had suddenly become wide-awake.

"Yes."

I turned around and stuck my head in Gracie's room. "How do you know that?" I asked, realizing I had completely forgotten about the all-important stocking stuffers. I hadn't stuffed the stockings in previous years and no one ever noticed. My kids had been so focused on all the presents under the tree that they never noticed their stockings were empty.

"My teacher at school said Santa stuffs the stockings with candy and toys," Gracie said firmly.

"Oh, boy!" Jack sat up in bed and clapped his hands, "Santa's leaving us candy and presents."

"Time for bed everyone," I said, realizing that I should be fired as Santa's elf. If those stockings weren't filled in the morning, the Big Man was going to look bad, and it would be my fault.

I walked down the hall and into the living room, where the stockings were hanging from the fireplace mantle. Filling stockings was the last thing I wanted to think about. I had to prepare for the 20 people who would be descending on my home for Christmas dinner the next day.

I turned my attention to getting things ready for the next day's dinner. I started by retrieving all the large platters that were stashed in various closets. As I opened the last closet to get my huge meat platter, I saw a solution to the stocking dilemma. On the top shelf were the kids' Halloween bags. They had gotten so much candy for Halloween that we were rationing it. Eventually, I had forgotten the bags were up there and the kids must've assumed they'd finished it all. I reached up and grabbed the bags, and dumped the contents out on the dining room table. I picked out the candy that didn't have telltale Halloween wrappers on it and stuffed it into the kids' stockings. If it didn't have a pumpkin or a witch on the wrapper, it ended up in the stockings.

Next, Santa's two big helpers headed up to the attic to bring down the toys. I looked over all the presents I had gotten for the kids to see if there was anything small enough to shove in a stocking, but I was out of luck. It was going to be candy-filled stockings this year.

After doing some work in the kitchen to prepare for my guests the next day, it was off to bed. I was pretty pleased with myself as I got under the covers. The kids wouldn't be completely disappointed because they'd have their candy-filled stockings, Scott and I would be well rested because I had done all the toy assembly weeks ago, and Christmas would be wonderful.

Christmas morning went beautifully and everyone was happy with their candy and their presents. Still, something seemed not quite right to me. I had promised myself I wouldn't go overboard on the kids' presents, but it looked as though things were missing. I could've sworn I'd bought more gifts than that. I shook my head and dismissed the thought because the kids were thrilled, and it was obvious Santa had come through once again.

One day, months later, I asked the kids if they wanted to fly kites. It was a windy day and perfect for a kite. They excitedly followed me to the closet in Scott's office where we kept the kites. I hardly ever ventured into there—if you saw his office you'd know why—it's not a place for a compulsively neat person. I put my hand on the closet handle and tugged. It was locked. Why was it locked?

"What's the matter, mommy?" Jack asked.

"The door is locked and I don't know . . ." I stopped in midsentence. I suddenly remembered why the door was locked. Before Christmas I had placed some wrapped gifts in this closet so I wouldn't have to carry them up to the attic. "Hey kids, would you do me a favor please?" I asked, trying to think of some way to get them out of the office so I could get the kites.

"Whaaaat, Mommy? I want to fly kites," Jack whined.

"Would you ah . . . ah . . . ah . . . both go to the front door and see if there's a package there?" Lame, but it was all I could think of. My kids love to announce when packages come to the house.

They went running out of the office. I reached up to the door casing and felt for the key I had hidden back when I'd hidden the presents. Then I opened the door and saw a stack of wrapped gifts. I grabbed the kites, slammed the door, and locked it.

Early the next morning while the kids were still asleep, I took the presents out of the closet, unwrapped them, then rewrapped them with birthday paper. I was all set for Jack and Gracie's birthdays that spring and summer.

Spring came and Jack, whose birthday is in April, was the first to enjoy his presents. It did seem a bit odd that one of his gifts was a pair of Mickey Mouse mittens and a wool hat at that time of year, but I told him that Tennessee weather could be very unpredictable.

With spring comes my annual obsession to clean and reorganize closets and drawers. I decided to start with the closet in my workout room. This is the catch-all closet that holds all the stuff we don't know what to do with. I opened the closet and started yanking stuff out when what do you know, I spotted some little boxes wrapped with Christmas paper. Yup, I had apparently stashed a few more presents in that closet as well. I must have been like a squirrel hiding acorns last Christmas.

Concerned that maybe in my determination to buy, wrap, and hide Christmas toys so early, I had placed others elsewhere, I went on a hunt. I checked every closet, looked through the garage, in drawers, in the garden shed, and even above the kitchen cabinets.

The only other things I came up with were an old camera I thought I had lost, some dead spiders, long-lost puzzle pieces, a Sippy cup lid, a fuzzy lollipop, and 20 dollars.

I vowed to become one of those last-minute shoppers. I also promised myself I would keep a list on my computer of Christmas present hiding places. Finally, I decided Scott shouldn't be denied one of the joys of fatherhood. From now on, I was going to hand him the tool set and the unassembled toys on Christmas Eve.

We'll Take the Stupid One

By Kae

Any time you leave the house with three kids—and a husband who's basically a big kid—with a credit card and keys to the car, you could have a problem. In that vein, let me give you a small piece of advice: Never, ever, take your whole family to get the tires rotated on your car.

On a beautiful spring day, we took our car to the shop to have the tires balanced and rotated. When I made the appointment, they guaranteed it would not take more than an hour to accomplish this. I explained that I was going to have to entertain my kids aged five, three, and one, and their father. They assured me the car would be ready in less than one hour.

Next door to the shop was a casual family restaurant, and David suggested a family lunch outing. I thought it was a perfect idea, so we dropped off the car and walked across the parking lot to the restaurant. Matthew and David started playing the basketball game in the back of the restaurant, so it was an hour and a half before we got back to the shop to pick up our car. I noticed right away that our car was hanging four feet off the ground with nothing that resembled tires on the wheels. Mr. Tire Rotator gave us a song and dance about a sudden and inexplicable inner tube accident and said we could wait another 45 minutes in their waiting room. The waiting room was filled with other less-than-happy people who were 45 minutes behind schedule and didn't look like they would enjoy spending the next five minutes, much less the next 45, with three kids and their fidgety father.

As an alternative to the waiting room, we decided to walk up and down the strip mall next door and look in all the windows. About four storefronts into the walk, we came upon a pet shop. "Can we go in, Daddy?" was the chorus from the two who could talk. So in we went. I was thinking we would look at some fish, a rabbit, or a gerbil or two. The kids and David would be completely entertained for the 45 minutes we had to kill. There were no other customers in the store and the owner was thrilled to have us. She showed the kids all the different mammals, birds, and amphibians. Then she led them to the wall of puppy cages. One cage was full of tiny Yorkshire Terrier puppies. Matthew and Christina stood and laughed at the puppy antics. Leaning down to the kids, the extremely crafty store owner asked, "You guys want to play with the puppies?" This was met with excited giggles and, "Yeah, let them out."

The owner opened the cage door and out tumbled eight fuzzy, pink-tongued little puppies the size of small bunny rabbits. Matthew and Christina were sitting on the floor and were promptly attacked by the little fuzz balls. Jessica was standing at my feet clapping her little hands and giggling.

One little pup came bounding up to Jessica and jumped up on her legs. To my dismay, Jessica reached down and grabbed the poor puppy by his ears and lifted him off the ground. His little body dangled down and his legs pumped furiously at the air. Jessica drew the little puppy up to her face and kissed him right on the lips with a big loud smacking sound. Then she tossed the dog away from her. He flew through the air, hitting the ground like a fuzzy ball, and rolled head over heels across the floor. The natural reaction would have been for the puppy to give Jessica a wide berth from then on, but instead he jumped to his feet and ran right back to Jessica and put his paws up on her legs.

It was not my intention to rotate the tires and come home with a puppy, but I turned to the store owner and said, "We'll take the stupid one."

Jail

By Pam

In preschool, Gracie was known for being well-behaved and cooperative. She was a teacher's dream. I was thrilled to see my daughter blossoming in school. She looked forward to going to preschool, loved learning, and was long past any separation anxiety issues.

One week, I had to travel out of town for four days to teach at a conference. My husband took care of the kids, including the job of driving Gracie to and from preschool. I arrived home early enough on Thursday to pick Gracie up. I walked into Gracie's class and, as I'd hoped, she ran to me, threw her arms around my waist and hugged me with all her might. Her teacher then walked over and asked if she could speak with me privately. The expression on her face was very solemn. Had my well-behaved child bitten someone? Exposed any private parts? Picked her nose?

"Is something wrong?" I asked, preparing to be told my daughter had done something in gross violation of preschool etiquette.

"Gracie seemed very sad this week with you not here. She was even quieter than she normally is and wasn't interested in playing with the other kids," the teacher said. "I asked her what was making her so sad and she said it was because you were gone."

"Well, that's understandable," I said, but from the look on the teacher's face I could tell there was more to it.

"Mrs. Bennett, Gracie was concerned because she said you were . . ." she began, but looked away before finishing her sentence. She looked down at her hands and whispered, ". . . in jail."

I must not have heard her correctly. "Did you say jail?" I asked, sure I was mistaken.

"Yes," nodded the teacher, obviously uncomfortable.

"Jail?" I asked again.

"I had a feeling she was mistaken," the teacher said, "but I wanted to make sure you knew about it."

She had a feeling she was mistaken? Did that mean she thought the possibility existed that I had been in the slammer?

"I was teaching at a conference," I replied, trying not to sound defensive.

The teacher smiled. "I figured it was probably something business-related, but you never know."

You never know?

I thanked the teacher for informing me what Gracie had said, and then I left with my daughter.

On the ride home, I asked her why she thought I was in jail. She didn't have an answer and retreated into typical three-year-old babble about her activities at school and what she wanted to eat for a snack when we got home. I explained to her precisely what jail was and how Mommy and Daddy have never been to jail and have no intention of ever going to jail. I also explained, as I had done before I left, why I had to go out of town. She said she understood and then started another conversation that let me know our current discussion was concluded.

That night, after the kids were in bed, my husband and I had a good laugh about Gracie's explanation of my whereabouts. I assumed this would be a one-time event and that Gracie would quickly forget about it. She, however, had other plans. She had either stumbled upon something that could cause her mother immense embarrassment whenever she said it, or she was truly convinced that I'd been incarcerated.

Her story didn't stop at preschool. The teacher and class in her church preschool were treated to the saga of how Mommy spent a week in jail. She even confided to the cashier at the supermarket that the reason we were buying ice cream was because I'd missed it while I'd been in jail.

All I could do was smile, shake my head, and explain that I hadn't been in jail, but I wonder how many people secretly believed it might be true. The cashier did seem to look at me more carefully. Perhaps he'd begun to assume that I was a shoplifter and had stuffed a pork roast under my sweatshirt.

Despite repeated serious discussions about the importance of telling the truth, making sure my daughter understood what jail really was, and inflicting punishment (in the form of time-out for every mention of jail), I continued to hear Gracie relate the story. Her friends in her playgroup were told, as were the mothers who stood nearby. Even the nurse in the pediatrician's office became privy to the sad day Mommy was hauled off to the lockup.

This had to end. Gracie had logged hours in time-out, I had taken numerous toys away from her, and I was ready to drop her off at the county jail myself so she could experience it firsthand. Realizing this was not appropriate Mommy behavior, I sat down next to her on the bed and repeated the importance of not telling stories that weren't true. I hadn't been to jail, and it wasn't nice to tell people that. She was hurting my feelings, I explained, and no one likes it when things are said about them that aren't true. Then something magical happened. Gracie looked up at me and saw a tear slowly rolling down my cheek. She reached over, touched the tear, and then put her arms around me.

"I'm so sorry," she said while hugging me. "I won't ever tell anyone about jail again."

She was true to her word. She never mentioned it from that moment on. Although I was very relieved, to this day I'm still not sure what happened. Did she think I was crying because she had told a hurtful lie? Or did she think I was crying because I was embarrassed about having been in jail? Regardless, we never spoke of it again.

Two years later, during "career day" in school, I found out Gracie had told everyone her mommy was a rock star.

"Why did you say that, Gracie?" I asked. "You know I'm a cat behaviorist."

"I know," she shrugged, "but that's boring. Being a rock star is more interesting."

At least it's better than jail.

Broken Wings

By Kae

On Cinco de Mayo the year Jessica turned five, David and I heard the words that to this day strike terror in our hearts: "Jessica has had an accident. We called an ambulance."

Running into the gymnastics center, I found my little five-year-old firecracker lying on the mats below the uneven bars. It was clear even to my untrained eye that there was something horribly wrong. No one's arms, no matter how flexible they are, should be going in that many directions at the same time.

There is no way to know how you will handle a real crisis until it happens. When I saw my child lying there in pieces, I knew I had to be calm and confident for her sake and for the sake of all the other little girls who had witnessed the accident. I rushed to Jessica's side. She was fully alert and, other than arms akimbo, seemed okay. I kissed her face and whispered in her ear, "Are you scared?"

"I think I did something really, really bad. They won't let me get up." Her little voice quavered but no tears leaked from her beautiful, big, brown eyes. Years later she told me the only reason she didn't cry that day was because it was a rule that if you were going to cry you had to go to the kitchen. Since she couldn't get up, she wasn't going to cry, no matter how scared she was, because she wasn't a baby and wasn't going to break the rules.

"Well, you're done with the scary part now. When the ambulance gets here we're going to go to the hospital and the doctors will make it all better. Okay?"

"Okay."

Apparently, they had been in line to go on the uneven bars, Jessica in front of Christina. They were working a drill where they stood on the low bar and jumped to the mat. Jessica misunderstood the drill. She thought she was supposed to jump to the high bar and hang there. Unfortunately, the high bar was set too far away to do that. She jumped, hit her hands on the high bar, and fell backward.

The number one golden rule of gymnastics: Never, never, never put your hands behind you when you fall. The human elbows are not designed to take much pressure before they snap. But she'd put both arms behind her when she'd fallen. She dislocated her right arm above and below the elbow. She dislocated her left elbow below the joint and fractured the bone above the elbow.

It would have been terrifying enough if Jessica were my only child in crisis. But Christina was there too, shaking and white as a sheet. David stayed with Jessica, telling her it was going to be okay, while I went to Christina and pulled her into my arms.

"Everything's going to be okay. Don't panic, okay." I said this not only to Christina but to the other girls standing in the group, as well.

I went back to Jessica and stroked her hair, keeping up an inane string of babble until the ambulance came. The paramedics took her vital signs and put her on a backboard with a collar around her neck in case she did more damage than was evident. They loaded her into the ambulance, and I jumped in the back. The ambulance took off toward the emergency room as the paramedic in the back continued to monitor her condition. He watched her intently: He said he was concerned that she'd go into shock. We bounced down the road and crossed the railroad tracks.

"Mommy, we're going the wrong way."

"Jessica, the ambulance driver knows how to get to the hospital," I said, trying to reassure her.

"No, Mommy, we're going the wrong way," she insisted.

"What makes you think that?" Jessica has a way of saying things with such authority and confidence that even though she was only five, I was compelled to peek out the back window just to double check.

"Because we live by the hospital and we never go over the railroad tracks to get home."

"Well, they probably know a shorter way." I was trying to be reassuring. It was somewhat surreal, riding in an ambulance with a broken five-year-old who was arguing about whether we were headed in the wrong direction.

"Fine, we just won't get there then," Jessica said in the tone of voice that would be followed by her folding her arms across her midsection if they weren't currently strapped to a backboard.

The paramedic looked at me and said, "I don't think we have to worry about her being in shock."

To Jessica's amazement, we made it to the hospital. She was unloaded and wheeled down a corridor to a private exam room. Several doctors and nurses started the process of assessing her. They didn't need an X-ray to see that her arms were a mess. The ER doctor called the orthopedic surgeon.

Then the doctor and nurse began to discuss how to get her out of her little green leotard. The conversation had again taken a surreal turn. I told them calmly that it was okay with me if they just went ahead and cut the leotard off her. What I really wanted to do was scream at these two medical miracles that I just needed them to fix my broken child and I could give a flip what happened to the silly little strip of spandex she was wearing.

Finally, the orthopedic surgeon came in and ordered her to be prepped for surgery. She was still awake and seemed calm. Her only complaints were that her nose itched and that she'd missed dinner.

A nurse came in and explained that they would have to start an IV line for the surgery and to give her some pain medication. Since both of her arms were out of commission, the only option for the IV was in her foot. The nurse told me it can be painful and if Jessica didn't hold still, they might have to try several times to get the line in. I could tell by the grim look on the nurse's face that she was not looking forward to wrestling with a five-year-old screaming monster while trying to hit a tiny vein in her foot with a giant needle.

"Okay Peepers, here's the deal," I began. (Peepers is my pet name for Jessica because she has such huge brown eyes.) "The nurse has to put a needle in your foot so you can get some medicine. It might hurt but you have to be really, really still so they can get it done the first time. Okay?"

"Okay."

I cradled her head in my hands and kissed her forehead while the nurse started putting in the IV. Jessica stayed perfectly still and the grim-faced nurse got the IV in on the first try. They immediately administered a powerful dose of pain medication, and my daughter drifted off to sleep. Once I knew she was completely under and wouldn't wake up until after the surgery, I excused myself, went down the hall to the ladies room, closed and locked the door, and threw up.

I waited in the little private room they had set aside for Jessica in the emergency room. Time seemed to stand still. It seemed like an eternity before David rushed in. In reality, he had broken all land speed records getting from the gymnastics center with Christina to the baseball field to pick up Matthew, back to our house to pack their overnight bags, and then off to my friend Debbie's house, where the kids would spend the night.

The surgery was supposed to take at least six hours. The surgeon said Jessica's arms would have to be opened at the elbow joints and the repairs made from the inside. The tip of one elbow was near her wrist bone. It was not a good prognosis. The arm had been broken across a growth plate. We would have to wait to see how that turned out as she grew.

David and I were escorted to the waiting room, where we broke down and sobbed in each other's arms. Three hours after the surgery began, I saw the surgeon walking down the hallway toward us. My heart leapt to my throat. I feared this was it, a mother's worst nightmare: My child had died under the anesthesia. Probably because he saw the look of terror on my face, or just because all went well, he smiled. Relief washed over me.

"Jessica did fantastic. We didn't have to open her elbows. Because she was all lean muscle, she pulled back together like a macaroni doll. We had to put a pin in her left arm at the break, but the piece of bone by her wrist slid right back into place through the same tissue tunnel it created during the fall. We're going to keep her in the hospital for the next day or two. She'll need physical therapy after the casts come off, but all in all, she's a lucky little lady."

David and I stayed with her in her hospital room all night, sitting in chairs in the corner. I watched the bed sheet over her little chest rise and fall with each breath she took. I dozed in and out. Every hour or so, a nurse came in and checked Jessica's blood pressure using a cuff on her leg.

"I'm hungry, I'm thirsty, and my nose itches," were the first words out of her mouth when she woke up the morning after the surgery.

"Oh, so you are awake. That's good." The nurse gave she a sweet smile while pulling the blood pressure cuff off of her tiny little leg.

"You keep waking me up pinching my leg," she informed the nurse.

The nurse checked her vital signs and scribbled them on her chart, then hung it on the end of the bed. She gave her some water from the pitcher that sat on a table next to the bed. "I'll bring you some juice and a breakfast tray."

I fed Jessica for the first time since she was old enough to hold a spoon. She ate everything on the breakfast tray and drank two containers of orange juice.

The nurse informed us that the surgeon expected Jessica to stay in the hospital for at least one more night. David went home to take a shower, gather clean clothes and toothbrushes, and get Jessica's special blanket—her "kankie." Before he came back to the hospital, he went to Debbie's to check on the kids and let everyone know Jessica was going to be okay.

A little bit later, the regular breakfast server brought in another tray of food. Jessica ate everything on this tray, too, and slurped more orange juice. The doctor made his rounds midmorning. He looked at her chart with a bemused look on his face.

"Well young lady, are you ready to go home?"

"Yes. That nurse kept waking me up all night pinching my leg. I want to go home and sleep in my own bed."

When David arrived with our much-needed personal items, he had Matthew, Christina, and my best friend's daughter, Big Jess (as she was affectionately known in our family) in tow. Everyone wanted to see Jessica for themselves to make sure she was really okay. It was Saturday morning. The gymnastics team practiced every Saturday morning, and—to my horror—Christina was wearing her yellow team leotard.

"I don't think it is a good idea for you to go to gymnastics today," I said. Fear knotted so tightly in my stomach I could barely stand erect.

"But I want to go. I didn't get hurt," Christina said matter-of-factly.

What I wanted to do was wrap all three of my children in bubble wrap, set them on the sofa in the family room, and never let them leave the house again for any reason. What I wanted to do was keep all three of my children right beside me, holding my hand so I could make sure nothing like this ever, ever happened again.

What I did was let Christina go to gymnastics. I let her go because I didn't want to take the chance that I would raise children who were afraid. I wanted to give them a chance to develop their own fears—not be loaded down with mine.

When we finally took Jessica home from the hospital, her arms were bandaged with temporary splints wrapped with copious amounts of cushioning material, all held together with stretchy gauze. The splints ended near her hands but the gauze continued for a couple of feet, effectively creating ribbons that could be used to tie her arms above her head. The surgeon and the nurse told us it was imperative that she keep both her arms elevated above her head for the next week, even when she was asleep. This would prevent swelling, they explained—swelling that could cause the circulation to her fingers to be compromised. We were to constantly monitor her fingers for the slightest color of blue—a telltale sign of poor circulation—and call the doctor's office immediately if we saw it. If all went well, she would get permanent casts on both arms after a week.

On the ride home, David lifted Jessica gently into the middle of the second row of seats of our Chevy Suburban. Then we tied her arms to the hand-holds at the top of each of the doors. I strapped the seat belt across her tiny little waist and pulled to make sure it was nice and snug.

When we got home, we piled her on the couch in our family room, surrounded by her favorite pillow, her stuffed animals, and her kankie.

Because she couldn't bend her elbows, it was impossible to get her into one of her own shirts. I confiscated one of David's T-shirts and turned it into a nightgown. The armholes were big enough to get the splints through, and it was long enough to almost reach the floor.

Our next order of business was to figure out how to keep her arms above her head. She was too weak to hold them there herself and refused to stay lying down so that we could prop them up on pillows. She wanted to be sitting up. Then David had a flash of brilliance. He went up to the attic and returned with our six-foot aluminum ladder. We put the ladder behind the couch and the tied the ends of her temporary splints to the appropriate rungs. It was the perfect solution. If she wanted to lie down, we just moved the ladder and tied her arms to a lower rung.

All the girls on the gymnastics team and the coaches came to see her, starting a few days after she came home. In our family room they found a tiny little girl wearing an outrageously oversized T-shirt with her tufted arms tied to an aluminum ladder, looking as if she were signaling a perpetual field goal. If anyone peeked in the windows, they might have assumed we were holding this child hostage.

For Jessica, one of the coups of the whole experience was that she got to watch unlimited TV. Since her arms were completely out of commission, there wasn't much else she could do. A five-year-old without activities is like a time bomb waiting to go off. She never complained about pain, but I gave her pain medication after lunch so she would go to sleep a few hours each day.

After a week, we went to the doctor to get her arms X-rayed and have her permanent casts put on. The X-rays showed she was healing exceptionally well. We walked out of the doctor's office with a bright pink cast on her left arm and a splint wrapped with an ace bandage on her right arm. We went home and put the ladder back in the attic.

Over the next week, Jessica became antsy at being cooped up in the house, so I took her for a walk around the block. "I want to go roller-skating," she whined as we walked down the street.

"You can't go roller-skating. If you fall down, you don't have any arms to catch yourself with."

"I'll just fall on my butt."

"Our luck, you'll fall directly on your face. Then you'll have two broken arms and a broken nose. Do you know how hard it'll be to hang you from the ladder by your nose holes?" She rewarded me with a brief giggle before she resumed arguing.

"Okay, if I can't go roller-skating, I want to go to the gym."

"What do you think you are going to do at the gym?"

"We were working on cartwheels, but I already know how to do those. I could work on aerials." For those of you who didn't spend three to four days a week for 15 years sitting in a gymnastics center, an aerial is a cartwheel where no hands touch the floor. When learning this skill, the hands are what keep the face from smashing into the mats. Once again, too much of a chance of finding my daughter hanging from a ladder by her nostrils.

The next morning she and I were sitting at the table in our kitchen, a full bowl of Cheerios in front of her and a much-needed cup of coffee in front of me. I was getting ready to spoon a mouthful of Cheerios into her mouth when the need to use the bathroom overwhelmed me.

When I came back into the kitchen, I was amazed to see that she'd figured out a way to contort her right arm—the one in the splint—so she could pick up the spoon and feed herself. A few Cheerios had escaped their destination, but basically, she was doing a great job. Jessica hates soggy cereal, so once the milk went in, it had to be eaten right away. When I left her in the kitchen with her bowl of Cheerios getting soggier by the moment, she decided to figure out a way to eat them before they were ruined.

"I'll feed you if you want me to," I said.

"I was too hungry to wait. Besides, I'm not a baby. You don't have to feed me." She continued to work at it until she figured out how to keep her shoulders down low so her mouth would stay closer to the bowl.

"I didn't think you were a baby, you silly. I was feeding you because you have two broken arms," I said, ruffling her brown hair.

After that, she ate on her own. She eventually figured out how to get dressed by herself. She even kept up with her schoolwork. She figured out how to hold one of those oversized pencils kindergarten children use to learn to write. Her handwriting was atrocious, but no one was complaining.

One week after her permanent casts were put on, her class was going on a field trip to the zoo. She was very upset that she'd miss it. David felt so bad that he contacted the teacher, found out the arrangements, and drove Jessica to Nashville to spend the day at the zoo with her classmates. He'd figured if she got too tired, they could have easily slipped away and come home early.

"Mommy, Mommy, guess what I got to do?" Jessica bounded into the kitchen when they got home.

"Whoa, slow down a little bit. You're scaring me to death running around like that," I said, turning from the dinner I was making. "What did you get to do?"

"Me and Daddy rode on an elephant." Her big brown eyes glittered with excitement.

"What!" My eyes must have been as big as saucers. My heart pounded in my chest. How stupid could David be? What if she had fallen? Elephants are really tall animals. She could have killed herself.

"We got to climb up this ladder and then me and daddy got to sit in a box on top of the elephant. When it walked, the box moved back and forth like this." She did her best imitation of how the box moved as the huge animal lumbered its way around the fenced area.

Seeing how excited she was made me relax a little bit. It was clear she never had felt the least bit scared.

"I hope that elephant didn't start running with you bouncing around in a box on its back. You could have fallen out onto the dirt and gotten smooshed under its big feet."

"Don't be silly, Mommy. Daddy was holding onto me." She went skipping out of the room in search of Matthew and Christina.

After eight weeks of casts and X-rays, it was finally time for the casts to come off. I knew that the surgeon was going to take the pin out of her arm in his office, and I was not looking forward to it. In my mind, there was no way a pin that was pushed into your bone can come out without hurting more than a little bit.

"I sure hope you get to take the cast off today," I said to Jessica as we sat in the waiting room, waiting.

"Me too. It's itchy."

"It smells pretty bad, too."

"Not as bad as Matthew's feet."

"Almost as bad. It smells like little girl sweat and dirt."

"I tried to keep it all cleaned up."

"I know you did. Remember when we talked about the pin they had to put in your arm to keep the broken parts together?" She nodded. "If they take the cast off, they are going to have to pull the pin out too."

"Well, they can't just leave it in there 'til I'm all growed up."

"It might sort of hurt, you know."

"Don't worry, I'll be big. Besides, we can go to McDonald's if I don't cry, right?" My daughter was truly amazing.

The cast was sawed off, which caused Jessica just a little concern until the nurse put the blade against her own hand and then against Jessica's hand. Once Jessica confirmed that the saw wasn't going to cut her barely healed arm off, she was fine. "Do you want to keep it?" the nurse asked as the pink cast cracked off. (Until the day Jessica moved out of our house, the little bitty pink cast sat on the shelves in her bedroom surrounded by all her gymnastics medals and trophies.)

The doctor came in to pull the pin. "Okay, young lady, I'm going to take these pliers here. First I'm going to twist, then I will pull, and we'll be all done. Okay?"

As he gave this speech, several nurses filed into the room and surrounded the exam table. I knew they were there to help hold down the squealing, thrashing child.

"Are you ready?" the doctor asked Jessica.

I don't know who was more nervous, the doctor having to attack the kewpie-doll-eyed little girl or the little girl who was being attacked. In one quick motion, the doctor expertly grabbed the pin and before we knew it, the whole thing was finished. I was so proud of Jessica; she didn't even flinch.

Instead, she looked proud as a peacock when the doctor looked at her and said, "You're the bravest little girl I know. I have big football players who cry like babies when I take their pins out. I'm going to have you come over here and tell them how to do it."

She informed the doctor with dead seriousness, "Well, I'm not a baby."

Evidence

By Pam

As with any family, there are rules in our home and my children are aware of what they are. Of course, that doesn't always mean they follow them. In fact, one of the rites of passage for any child is to try to break a certain number of rules without getting caught.

The dilemma we face as mothers is lack of evidence. If you didn't see what happened and no one owns up to it, who gets the blame? The likeliest culprit? That doesn't seem fair. Should you use your best detective-like interrogation skills to try to trip someone up into telling the truth? Sometimes that works, but after a while the kids learn your tricks and are able to outwit you. Do you use guilt? Threats? Understanding and patience? Do you punish everyone?

In our house, I do my best to explain to my children that telling the truth and facing the consequences is much better than lying to cover up a crime. Being caught in a lie will automatically raise the severity of the punishment. My children know lying is wrong. They try very hard to tell the truth but sometimes they just can't seem to get out of their own way as they fumble for excuses and think they can put one over on mom. Sometimes it works; sometimes it doesn't. One night, being sneaky and not telling the truth came back and bit both my kids in the proverbial butt.

Of all the rules in our home, there are two that my children had particular difficulty following.

1. Do not touch anything on Mommy or Daddy's office desks without permission.

2. Jumping on the furniture isn't allowed. Our chairs and sofas are not to be used as trampolines.

Unfortunately, the setup in our sunroom was particularly tempting. We have a seating arrangement that includes a sofa with two large, upholstered chairs on either side. The sofa and chairs all face an upholstered ottoman. It was often very hard for my kids to resist leaping from the sofa or chairs, bouncing off the ottoman, and then landing with a thud on the carpet. For added fun, Gracie and Jack would spread out the throw pillows on the carpet as a landing pad.

The sunroom is at the back of our house, and my children always tried to time their gymnastic events for when I was on the opposite side of the house doing laundry, talking on the phone, or vacuuming. As I was running the vacuum in the bedrooms I heard lots of loud, cackling laughter, but as soon as I turned the machine off, everything got suspiciously quiet. That's when I tiptoed into the sunroom to try to see what was going on. I found my kids sitting on the sofa with big, innocent smiles on their faces. The telltale signs that they had not been in that quiet position for long were the huffing and puffing, red faces, and pillows tossed askew on the sofa.

One day Gracie came running up to me. "Mommy, Mommy," she said excitedly as she pulled at my shirt while I was putting dirty clothes in the washer. "The lamp in the sunroom fell near Jack."

"Is he all right?" I asked as we both raced down the hallway toward the sunroom.

"I think so," she answered.

Sure enough, lying on the carpet, right behind the sofa, was one of the end table lamps. Sprawled out next to the lamp was Jack. "Jack, what happened? Are you hurt?"

"No," he answered as he got up. "Let's go play in your bedroom, Gracie."

Normally, my son is not the least bit stoic. If a feather landed on his head he would turn on the waterworks and complain of severe pain. Jack was dramatic. He could cry at the drop of a hat, and he loved sympathy. So the fact that he had just been in some kind of altercation with a heavy lamp and was not the least bit concerned led me to one conclusion: He caused the lamp to fall and didn't want any more discussion about it.

"Wait a minute," I said as he tried to walk past me. "How did the lamp end up on the carpet?"

Both kids offered blank stares.

"Were you jumping on the sofa or the chairs?" I asked while looking directly at Jack.

Jack shook his head. Now, normally, Gracie would have loved to rat on her brother, since being a tattletale is truly one of the high points of sibling life. The fact that she didn't offer up anything led me to believe she was in on the action and that implicating Jack would mean she'd also have to implicate herself.

"So," I said, "I'm to believe that the lamp simply fell all by itself off the table?"

Jack and Gracie nodded and smiled. They liked this possibility. No one would be to blame if the lamp simply took it upon itself to leap from the table onto the carpet.

"If the lamp fell all by itself," I continued, "then how did you end up right next to it, Jack?"

Jack looked over at Gracie for help, but she was staring straight ahead.

"I was standing there behind the sofa, and the lamp just landed on me."

"Oh, I see," I said while scratching my chin as if trying to piece together the puzzle. "You just happened to be standing in the exact spot where the lamp fell."

Jack nodded enthusiastically, overjoyed at the possibility that this explanation would do the trick.

"And no one was jumping on the furniture at all, right?" I asked.

Both kids shook their heads. They were sticking to their story.

I replaced the lamp on the table, fluffed the pillows on the sofa, and gave my children another lecture about why it's dangerous to jump on the furniture. They said they understood, and even though they promised me they hadn't been anywhere near that lamp, they would never, ever jump on the furniture in the future.

One week later, while the family was seated at the dining room table for dinner, Scott started talking to me about a house he was working on where he was doing some very intricate wood trim. Instead of trying to describe it, he decided to go into his office and retrieve his digital camera to show me some pictures of his work. He turned on the camera and handed it to me.

"Wow, that's beautiful, Scott," I said of the photo.

"Hit the arrow button, because there are more views of the trim," he said.

I pushed the button to advance to the next picture, and then pushed it again to keep advancing. Suddenly I wasn't looking at a picture of an unfinished house anymore. There on the screen was a picture of my son leaping off the back of the high-back upholstered chair in the sunroom. He was at least three feet in the air above the chair. I advanced the camera again and saw picture after picture of Jack taking flying leaps off the back of the chair. As I continued to look at these pictures I came to two very important conclusions.

1. Jack had, indeed, been leaping off the furniture.

2. Based on the poorly framed and focused picture, Gracie must have been the photographer.

I placed the camera on the table and turned toward my children. "Jack, have you ever jumped off the top of the chair in the sunroom?" I asked.

"No, Mommy," he said as he continued eating, totally unaware of what I was looking at in the camera. "We're not allowed."

"Gracie, you know the rule about never touching anything on Daddy's desk, right?" I asked.

"Sure," she responded.

"So you wouldn't take Daddy's camera without permission, would you?"

She shook her head and continued eating, then stopped for a moment, looked at me, looked at the camera on the table, and went back to eating her carrots as if they were her absolute favorite food in the world. Although Jack was totally unaware, Gracie had put the pieces together and realized she might not be able to talk her way out of this one.

"Jack and Gracie," I continued in a very casual tone, "do you know what the word evidence means?"

"No," they both responded.

"Well, you're about to."

The children have since learned why it's important never to lie—or at least to be smart enough to not leave any evidence behind!

Chapter 5

On a Wing and a Prayer

Magic Foo Foo Dust

By Kae

Before I became a mom, I was just a normal, slightly shorter, slightly thinner than average woman. I'm not really sure at what point the transition occurred, but one day I woke up and realized I was a superhero. My children looked to me with expectant eyes, trusting me when I said, "Jump into my arms, I'll catch you" or "Don't worry, I won't let you drown."

In the eyes of my children, I was the go-to gal when they had questions about how the universe functioned. I was the one who knew the names of every species of animal. I was the one who knew how all the planes, trains, and automobiles worked. I was the one who knew how the grass grew and why the sky was blue. I was the one who had the ear of the Easter Bunny, Santa Claus, and the Tooth Fairy.

In the eyes of my children, I became the superwoman who could lift two or more children into my arms and run like the wind to get out of a sudden rainstorm. I was the possessor of powers that could heal a boo-boo with a magic kiss, that could locate lost toys with my X-ray vision, that could make favorite blankets appear out of thin air. I was the brave and courageous mommy who eradicated flying insects and birds from their bedrooms. I was the mommy who never panicked, even when there was blood.

For a child, there are two realms of reality: light and dark. In the realm of light, children are courageous. Daylight hours are spent running around the house with makeshift capes tied around their necks saving siblings from make-believe bad guys, digging under beds to find lost socks or shoes, and going in basements to help carry down the laundry. In the realm of light, children are brave, independent souls. They declare their independence by dressing themselves, feeding themselves, telling their parents that they aren't babies and don't need any help putting on their shoes.

As soon as the last rays of sunlight leave the sky, we enter into the realm of the dark. Here, those same courageous children become little scaredy-cats. The same child who spent the day brandishing a pirate's sword and chopping off the heads of child-eating sharks refuses to go upstairs by himself to bring you a clean diaper for the baby. The child who commanded you away from her bedroom while she dressed herself for school (making you five minutes late for your own class) is the same child who refuses to go to the same bedroom and put on her pajamas. These are the same children who hid under their beds and in their closets during the afternoon game of hide-and-seek; but now that darkness has fallen, they refuse to let you leave their bedrooms until you have examined every inch of the closet, closing the door firmly, and have lain prone on the floor to make sure no monsters are hiding under the bed.

Although I had a wide array of super powers in my Mommy Arsenal, my strongest power was the ability to banish monsters and other creepy things that went bump in the night.

Every parent has been awakened in the wee hours by the terrified shrieking of their young child. According to the All the Goofy Advice About Babydom books in my reference collection, some children have nightmares, beginning around age two-and-a-half. It's the conventional wisdom that once the child reaches age six, the nightmares will subside on their own. Having three children each spaced two and a half years apart ensured that for many years it was a common occurrence in the Allen household to be awakened from a deep sleep by one of the three children screaming like a wild banshee.

Many a 2 a.m. would find me bolting from my bed, narrowly avoiding stubbing my naked toes on my metal bed frame, and stumbling down darkened stairs and hallways. Going into my children's rooms in the dark was always a risky business. If I weren't careful, I would find myself sliding precariously across the hardwood floor on the silken ear of a discarded toy bunny. Often, in my haste to aide my terrified child, I would find my feet tangled in a pile of clothing that the child had purposely placed directly in front of his or her door—a favorite booby trap set by the Allen children for nighttime prowlers. It is amazing how slippery the combination of a hardwood floor and a child's silky underpants with ruffles on the butt can be.

Once I was awakened in the middle of the night by Christina howling in her bedroom downstairs. I ran the obstacle course down the dimly lit stairs and up the hallway, and flew into her room, avoiding the pile of discarded clothing right at the last moment. I scooped her up and held her trembling little body close to mine while crooning comforting sounds in her ear. Finally she began to relax in my arms. We lay together in the bed, Christina snuggled up to me, as I stroked her hair until she finally calmed down.

"Stay here and sleep with me, Mommy," Christina pleaded as I got up to go back to bed.

"I can't sleep here, Christina. I have to go upstairs and sleep with Daddy," I said as I stood and tucked the covers under her little body.

"Are the monsters going to get Daddy too?" Her eyes were wide with concern.

"There aren't any real monsters. They were just in the dream in your head," I said, smoothing down her blonde hair and tapping her forehead with my index finger.

"Nope, they're here. They're gonna' come back soon as you leave and I'm alone." She trembled under the covers again. I sat back down on the bed.

"Christina, there are no real monsters in this house. If we had a monster, Cindy would go crazy and eat them all up." (Cindy was our Labrador Retriever–Chow mix.)

"Cindy can't see these monsters. They're people monsters, not dog monsters," she informed me with earnest blue eyes.

This situation called for drastic action. I reached into the pocket of my pajama pants and made a big show of using my hand to look around for something. "I thought it was in this pocket," I mumbled. "Nope, not in this one, maybe in the other one," I said as I dug around in my other pocket.

"What're you looking for, Mommy?" Christina was now sitting up, watching me intently.

"Oh, here it is," I said. I pulled my closed fist out of my pocket as if I were holding something. "In my hand I have something very, very special." I showed her my closed hand.

"What is it?"

"Foo foo dust."

"What's foo foo dust?"

"It's a special dust that keeps the people and dog monsters away. It is very powerful and no monsters in the universe can get by it."

She was up on her knees now, trying to see into my hand.

"Lie down and get under your covers so I can sprinkle the magic foo foo dust around you on your bed. That way no monsters will be able to get you."

Christina crawled back under the covers and settled in. I made a big show of sprinkling the foo foo dust around her on the bed and even went back into my pocket for a little bit more just for good measure. I kissed her on the forehead and went back to bed for a blissfully uninterrupted night of sleep.

The next day, the news of the magic monster-repelling foo foo dust made the rounds among the Allen children. During the period of nightmares a nightly ritual emerged. Each child would crawl into bed and pull the covers up to their chest. David would go in and give them their "Daddy water." The next step was for me to come in, dig in my pocket for magic foo foo dust, and sprinkle the beds to keep the monsters away.

The foo foo dust did the trick as far as keeping the monsters out of the children's rooms at night. One unintended consequence of sprinkling a ring of monster-repelling foo foo dust on the children's beds was that they did not want to break the ring by getting out of bed before morning. I actually count this as a parental coup. Not only did we banish the monsters, but we also never had to worry about the children getting up after we put them to bed for the night.

The Bodyguard

By Pam

I'm a pretty quiet, easygoing person (if you overlook the whole OCD thing) who is law-abiding and rule-following. I've never been a troublemaker and have a pretty spotless childhood record of always having been a good kid. Apparently, that didn't stop someone from deciding I was up to no good at Chuck E. Cheese.

Scott and I had brought the kids to Chuck E. Cheese as a reward for having been good all week. In our house, a trip to Chuck E. Cheese was the Triple Crown prize. They got pizza and soda; they got to play countless games in an attempt to win tickets that are redeemable for frighteningly overpriced junk; and it's the one public place where they could safely wander out of Mommy and Daddy's sight. They had to be top-notch, napkin-using, manner-displaying, room-cleaning, tantrum-less children all week to get the coveted trip to Chuck E. Cheese. Hold on, I just have to interrupt this story to let you all know that although I mope and frown over the fact my kids are getting older, I am overjoyed at the fact they've now outgrown the nightmare world of Chuck E. Cheese. I'm thrilled at not having to see that giant rat (excuse me, "mouse") walking around and patting my kids on their heads after patting 30 other kids' heads immediately beforehand (remember,

I'm the OCD half of the Two Loons). I'm glad I no longer have to carry a half-gallon of hand sanitizer because my kids touched the handle of a game three seconds after a sneezing, snot-filled kid just walked away from it. Oh, don't get me wrong – I know there are plenty of germs in the pre-teen world but I'm so glad Chuck E. Cheese and even the germ-filled indoor fast-food restaurant playgrounds are in my rearview mirror of mothering. Okay, I can get back to the story now.

As routine, we entered the restaurant and Scott, Jack, and Gracie stood with me at the cashier's post just long enough to get their game tokens. Then they were off and running. I stayed at the counter to order the pizza and drinks and pay for the tokens. I ordered our food and was putting the change in my wallet when the next woman in line stepped up to order. After ordering, the cashier handed her a plastic sign with a number on it, as she had just done with me, and said, "Place this on your table and your pizza will find you."

I chuckled when the cashier said that. It was a silly little joke the Chuck E. Cheese employees probably say hundreds of times a day, but it struck me as funny. The woman ordering the food, however, turned and glared at me. "Do you find me funny for some reason?" she asked in an icy tone.

I was taken off guard. "No, I was just laughing at what the cashier said. It was cute," I said as I finished putting my wallet back in my purse and started walking away.

"Don't you walk away from me," the woman said. "You were making fun of my accent because I'm not an American."

The woman had no accent so I had no idea what she was talking about, plus I was only laughing at the cashier's little joke—a joke that was starting to seem pretty unfunny at this point.

"Ma'am, I don't know what you're talking about. I was laughing at the cashier's joke. You must've misunderstood." I refused to apologize for something I didn't do, but I tried to be as nice as possible while removing myself from someone who obviously had some sort of chip on her shoulder. The cashier noticed the tension and immediately asked if she could help the next person in line. She didn't want to be a part of this, and I couldn't blame her.

"You better be careful," the woman said as she continued to follow me. "You don't know what I'm capable of."

I walked away quickly. I was getting a little scared, and I wanted to find Scott.

The woman walked to a table with her son and sat down. I thought this was the end of our encounter, so I placed my number at a table far away from her and went to find Scott. When I told him what happened, he said we'd keep an eye on things and leave if we had to. The kids were having a blast, and we didn't want to ruin their good time.

Our food arrived. We enjoyed our pizza, as much as one can enjoy pizza that tastes like cardboard, and went through a bucket of game tokens. I had forgotten all about the strange encounter with the woman.

Gracie asked to go to the restroom, so the two of us excused ourselves and headed in that direction. While in the stall helping Gracie onto the toilet, a voice suddenly bellowed, "Lady, I know you're in here." It was the familiar voice of wacko woman. "I'm warning you not to mess with me."

"Mommy, why is that woman mad at you?" asked Gracie as I helped her off the toilet and pulled her pants back on.

"She's confused, honey. It's okay," I said.

"Mommy, let's go, I'm done," Gracie said. She was anxious to get back to the game area. She tried to open the stall door but I put my hand over hers to stop her. I didn't want to frighten her, but I didn't want to go out there. I had never been in a fight in my life, and the first time certainly wasn't going to be in the bathroom at Chuck E. Cheese.

The woman started babbling more nonsense about how I had insulted her. I was scared. It was obvious this woman had problems, but why did she have to pick me? Of all the mothers at Chuck E. Cheese, why did it have to be me?

I took my cell phone out of my purse to call Scott and have him rescue me from the Chuck E. Cheese bathroom. I had no cell reception. No reception? In the past, I have had to endure listening to endless cell phone conversations echoing from inside the stalls next to me in public bathrooms, and yet the one time I really needed to use my own phone I had no reception? How unfair was that? Chalk that up to another reason to dislike Chuck E. Cheese.

Suddenly, I heard the bathroom door open and close. I peeked out through the gap in the stall door while being extremely careful not to actually touch my nose to the surface. She was gone. Thank goodness.

"Come on, Gracie, let's wash our hands."

After a quicker-than-I-would-normally-allow hand washing, it was time for Secret Agent Mommy to take over. I opened the restroom door just a crack and peered out. The coast was clear. Taking Gracie by the hand, we left the bathroom and silently inched our way through the restaurant. We tiptoed passed the drink dispensers and then darted behind the hammerheads game. The coast was clear, so we made our way to the basketball hoop game where there was enough cover for me to scope out the landscape. It was a long stretch across open ground to make it to the whack-a-duck game where Scott and Jack were. I took Gracie by the hand and tried to calmly stroll to my husband while keeping my secret agent eyes darting in all directions, on the lookout for the scary woman.

We decided to leave, but I thought I should inform the manager about the woman first. I left Gracie and Jack with Scott and I made my way, Secret Agent Mommy style, to the front of the restaurant. I asked to see the manager. When I told her what happened, she said she'd call mall security. I dashed back to Scott and the kids. I imagined a big, buff security guard walking into the restaurant to escort the woman off the mall property.

The mall security guard arrived a few minutes later. He looked all of 16 and incapable of evicting anyone older than a kindergartener. As the security guard went over to talk to the woman, I watched and waited. If he escorted her out, we'd stay and play. If he didn't, we'd leave.

The scrawny, teenage security guard–boy walked over to us and said wacko woman (okay, he didn't actually refer to her that way) would stay away from me. If I wanted to stay, he would stand with us for as long as we remained in the restaurant. He couldn't insist that she leave because she hadn't actually threatened me. Apparently, scaring the heck out of me didn't count.

"Thanks for the offer, but I think we'll just leave," I said to Opie the security guard. Then I turned to the kids and put on my best smile. "Okay, kids," I said in my most pleasant, we'll-have-a-better-time-somewhere-else voice, "I think it's time we head out of here."

"Please, Mommy, please, please, please can we stay?" whined Jack.

"Mommy, I was soooooooo good this week, please?" added my daughter.

"How about we go get some ice cream at Dairy Queen?" I offered. Dairy Queen was the second most coveted reward, after Chuck E. Cheese.

"They have ice cream here. Please can we stay?" Gracie pleaded. "We used our good manners all week."

She was right. They had earned this trip. I wasn't going to cut it short just because some scary woman had made me fear for my life. What kind of mommy was I anyway? Was I a mommy or a mouse? (no offense, Chuck E.) I would just make sure Gracie and I didn't consume any more soda so we wouldn't need to make trips to the bathroom.

We spent the rest of our time at Chuck E. Cheese with Opie, our own personal bodyguard. I appreciated the gesture but honestly, the guy was all of five feet, five inches tall and maybe weighed just a little more than Gracie. Wacko woman could've taken him out with one hand. It was also a bit weird to watch the other parents looking at us and whispering. I guess they wondered whether we were some kind of troublemakers. Now that I think about it, I did look pretty threatening in my yellow sweatshirt, white shorts, and yellow rubber sandals.

When it was time to leave, we all thanked Opie for making us feel safe during our daredevil visit to the giant rat's money-sucking germ factory (don't worry, I didn't actually say that—what kind of mother do you think I am?). Gracie and Jack waved to him as we headed out the door. Opie even stood at the door and watched to make sure we got to car safely. Opie may not have looked intimidating, but he sure was courteous.

We stayed away from Chuck E. Cheese for almost two months. I was in no hurry to go back there, but it never became an issue because my kids went on a bad behavior spree for several weeks. Time-outs were a daily occurrence for a while. By the time we did finally make it back to Chuck E. Cheese, I felt comfortable believing that the scary woman had moved on to harassing other people in other areas of town.

We were having a great time playing games and eating our cardboard pizza. Suddenly I felt someone tap me on the shoulder. I hesitantly turned around and saw two women smiling at me.

"Excuse me," one of them said. "We were here a of couple months ago when you were here. You had the security guard with you. Are you famous?"

Famous! How about that? I've become a celebrity at Chuck E. Cheese.

Thanks, Opie!

Blown Away

By Kae

David and I had dinner together for the first time in a restaurant called Fast Eddie's, which is near Sarasota at the northern end of a set of barrier islands that run down the western coast of Florida. The restaurant's slogan was "cold food, warm beer." We both loved it. We spent hours talking and getting to know each other. It has always been a cherished memory.

During one of our annual summer trips to Florida, we decided it would be fun to take the kids to the restaurant where we'd had our first dinner. Dressing the children to go out to eat was always interesting. First, Matthew would not want to change out of his play clothes. To him, it was perfectly acceptable to go out to eat wearing the same clothes you had been wearing to fish in the hot sun all day, using the seat of your pants as a rag to wipe squid guts on after you baited your hook. Even when we did manage to wrestle him into a clean pair of shorts and a clean shirt, we would always have to send him back to his room to change his underwear and socks.

The girls were easier because they loved to get dressed up. This was when Jessica insisted on wearing the exact same outfits as Christina. If Christina wore striped shorts, Jessica wore striped shorts. This matching game went all the way down to shoes, socks, and yes, even underwear. If Christina was wearing pink underwear, Jessica was going to wear pink underwear. If Jessica's pink underwear was dirty, no problem, she would just wear Christina's extra pair.

So this is how we left the condo for our trip to Fast Eddie's: Matthew complaining that his clean socks were scratching his feet, Christina in her cute little sundress with her light pink underwear, and her sidekick, Jessica, wearing the exact same sundress and an extra pair of Christina's light pink underwear.

Summertime in Florida is synonymous with thunderstorms. Every day, like clockwork, the afternoon thunderstorms roll in. Lightning flashes, thunder booms, the wind howls, and rain marches across the water in a wall of huge droplets. As soon as the storm has passed, the day once again turns sunny and gorgeous.

As we made our way north along the beach road, we watched the black clouds gathering over the Gulf of Mexico. The restaurant was right across the street from the beach. The parking lot behind the restaurant was a large, open space paved with crushed shells and sand. David parked the car at the far back of the parking lot, even though there were plenty of spaces in the front of the lot nearer the building. This parking technique was then and continues to be the bane of the existence of Allen family outings. It doesn't matter how many open spaces there are next to the building you want to go to, David will always park as far away as possible. In the beginning, I thought it was because he didn't want to ding the door on our new car. This excuse went the way of the dinosaur when our "new" car was ten years old with more than 100,000 miles on it, and I was still hiking from the far end of the parking lot.

We finally made our way into the restaurant and had a lovely dinner, regaling the kids with fond memories of our first dinner date, then turning the topic to all things kid. We finished our dinners, paid the bill, and headed out the front door for the long trek back to the car. As soon as we opened the door of the restaurant, we knew we had a problem. The dark clouds that were over the gulf when we went in were rapidly bearing down on us. As soon as we stepped off the porch of the restaurant onto the concrete strip of sidewalk, there was a loud clap of thunder. Matthew grabbed my right hand. Christina grabbed my left. This left David and Jessica on their own.

The wind began to howl around us. David, realizing the rain was mere seconds away, tried to scoop Jessica up into his arms. "No, I can walk myself," she declared. (Jessica was our most stubborn child. Her key phrase in her early years was, "I'm not a baby." If she even suspected that you intended to treat her like a baby, she would dig in her heals and wild dogs couldn't budge her.)

David and Jessica took the lead in our mad dash for the car. In the howling wind, Jessica's cute little sundress was billowing out behind her like a sail. Jessica was very, very thin—all long arms and long legs and not an ounce of fat. The wind kept catching in her dress, dragging her backward. David had his head down and was moving toward the safety of the car at a quick clip, towing Jessica and her billowing sundress sail behind him. I had Matthew and Christina by the hands and, with heads down, we were struggling against the wind. As we got to the edge of the parking lot, small pieces of sand and shells started stinging our legs. The kids and I quickened our pace, trying to get to the car before our legs were sandblasted to the bone.

The wind roared in my ears and thunder boomed all around. Matthew was huddled next to my side as close as he could get without knocking me down. I knew he was petrified of thunder, and I was therefore amazed when I realized that over the howl of the wind, I could hear him laughing.

David was so intent on making it to the car and unlocking the doors that he didn't notice Jessica was pulling at his hand yelling, "Stop, Daddy, stop!" He held tighter to her arm and kept tugging her forward, most likely thinking she was having trouble running against the wind. But she kept yelling, "Stop, Daddy, stop."

Hearing the distress in her voice, I looked up, squinting to keep the debris out of my contact lenses. I instantly saw what Matthew thought was so funny. The act of running to keep up with her daddy had dislodged Jessica's ill-fitting underpants. Then the wind had blown under her sundress and had dropped her pink underpants to her ankles. She was doing a rapid duck walk next to David, trying to keep up with his pace while shuffling in the limited constraints of the underpants' leg holes.

Finally, David heard her plaintive cries and looked down. In one swoop, he swept our daughter with her billowing sundress and underpants at her ankles into his arms. He ran the last few yards to the car, quickly unlocked the doors, and dove in. Matthew, Christina, and I ran the rest of the way to the car with bits of sand and seashells nipping into our calves. We all jumped into the car just as the big fat raindrops began to beat like a drum on the roof.

The Bennetts go on Vacation

By Pam

Before having children, vacations were wonderfully restful. After we had kids, though, Scott and I were unsure about what exactly might work as a family vacation. We had one very strong-willed daughter and one son who thought using his "inside voice" meant "pretend you're in a football stadium." But other families we knew managed to take vacations, and we were longing to get away. When my friend, Angela, and her husband took their five kids (all under the age of six) to Disney World, we knew we were being a couple of weenies. It was time to take a vacation.

Not quite ready for Disney World, but knowing that our kids, at three and almost five, would probably enjoy rides, games, and an array of non-nutritional food, we decided to head for Dollywood in nearby Pigeon Forge, Tennessee—just a three-hour drive away. This was going to be our practice vacation. If we did well with this one, we'd consider braving a longer distance in the near future.

We'd only be gone four days, but from the amount of stuff I packed, you'd think we were moving. Gone were the days of tossing a swimsuit, some cosmetics, and a couple changes of clothes into a suitcase for those adult vacations. When you have young kids, you must pack practically the entire contents of their rooms. You must pack three times as many clothes as you think they'll need because you always have to allow for food spills, bathroom mishaps, weather changes, and any unexpected fickle fashion fits. Then there are the toys. You have the car toys, toys for the hotel room in case of rainy weather, stuffed animals as sleep buddies, and the stuffed animals that would be lonely if left home by themselves when the other stuffed animals were on vacation.

Next came the food. We were going to be staying in a condo-style hotel, so we'd have our own kitchen. I thought that would be the easiest way to handle most of the meals if we were in a hurry to get to the theme park, or if the kids were too exhausted to eat in a restaurant at the end of the day. That, of course, meant packing lots of food. Packing lots of food meant buying coolers to put the food in. So the day before our vacation, I shopped.

That night, while my kids and husband relaxed in front of the TV, I stood in our bedroom with five suitcases open before me. Scott had done his share of the packing, which basically amounted to tossing a pile of his clothes, unfolded, into his suitcase. The rest of his suitcase was filled with magazines that he naively thought he'd have time to read. I didn't know what vacation he thought he was going on, but if he assumed he would have all this free time for reading, I wasn't going to burst his clueless bubble.

The next morning, as he did the typical manly thing of checking the car's oil, tire pressure, and windshield wiper fluid, I piled the filled coolers, toys, suitcases, pillows, DVDs, camera, video camera, and potty seats into a small mountain in the driveway. I had done all the packing so it was now Scott's turn to wedge everything in the minivan.

By the time I got the kids dressed, fed, and ready to hit the road, I was exhausted but ready for our first family vacation.

The kids were excited and we spent much of the car ride talking about all the rides we'd go on and the fun things we'd do. Everyone was psyched. When we arrived at the hotel, I brought the kids up to the room while Scott tackled the exhausting job of unloading the tightly packed car. With all the food put away and everyone rested and pottied, we were headed for our first day at Dollywood.

This was supposedly the week to be there, as they were advertising some sort of kids' festival that catered to very young children. It may have been the time to be there for the activities, but it sure wasn't the time to be there for the weather. Of course, we had no way of knowing this was the start of Tennessee's hottest summer. Temperatures were already in the high 90s and it was still morning.

After the initial "fun" of waiting on a long line just to get into the park, our day went downhill fast. My kids were afraid of almost every game where balloons popped, air guns went off, or large stuffed animals hung overhead in bizarre suspension. Thinking we might do better with the rides, we headed toward the ones meant for the younger set. Standing on a long line in 95-degree heat, only to be spun around in circles until you feel sick (literally) on the ride, was not my idea of a fun vacation. Those spinning teacup rides may look innocent enough with their bright colors and fun designs, but don't let that fool you: they're evil, vomit-inducing, torture mobiles. And even if you aren't sick enough from the ride to vomit, the sight of other kids getting sick will cause you to toss your cookies.

Because it was so hot, I was very concerned with keeping us all hydrated. We drank lots of water. We visited lots of bathrooms, and of course, my kids never had to go at the same time—that would have been far too convenient for Mommy. It was only after we were almost at the front of the line for a ride that one of my children would announce the need to pee.

Although I lugged my camera all around the park, I didn't take many pictures. My kids were cranky, hot, and obviously disappointed. I already had a large collection of pictures of my frowny-faced kids from previous outings. I didn't need to take more. They'd had a very different idea of what a vacation was supposed to be. Oh sure, I do have a few pictures of my sweaty husband helping my sweaty son eat his rapidly melting ice cream cone. Then there's the picture of my daughter standing outside one of the stores with her arms folded tightly across her chest, a serious pout on her face, and her lips sticking out like a duck's beak because Mommy wouldn't fork over 40 bucks for a cowgirl hat.

After lunch (which, mercifully, was in an air-conditioned restaurant in the park), I brought up the idea of calling it a day. Both my kids broke out in huge smiles. Their faces seem to sparkle for the first time all day—or maybe it was just residue of ice cream and cotton candy stuck to their cheeks. We had had all the "fun" we could handle that day and headed out of the park.

The parking lot shuttle ride to our car seemed twice as long and not nearly as comfortable as it had been that morning. Gracie was sitting in Scott's lap, half asleep, and Jack was completely asleep in my arms, adding a line of drool to the myriad of substances covering his face. I had run out of face wipes long ago—not that those flimsy little wipes could handle the Super Glue cotton candy sugar after it makes contact with skin.

Back at the hotel, everyone bathed and napped. The entire family was sound asleep by four in the afternoon. Whoopee, what a fun vacation!

After our naps, we decided to head for the hotel pool and relax, so the day wouldn't be a total loss. There were two pools at the hotel—one a completely unheated, totally frigid kiddie pool and the other a barely tolerable adult pool. Despite the oppressive heat, the kiddie pool was like sitting in a bucket of ice water. Luckily, we'd brought the kids' water wings so we could all enjoy the more tolerable adult pool. Gracie and Jack had a blast and it was wonderful to actually see smiles on their faces after our first vacation day disappointment. When it comes to Jack and Gracie, all they really need is water in order to have a good time.

Later that night, after we had put the kids to bed, Scott and I talked about the chances of day two at Dollywood being any better than day one. The most fun the kids had all day was in the pool, and if that were the case, why were we spending money on this vacation when we have a beautiful pool at home?

I went downstairs to the lobby and told the clerk we'd be checking out in the morning. He didn't even ask why. He was probably very familiar with the look on this exhausted and frustrated mom's face. When it comes to vacations, he was probably smart enough to know not to bring the kids. I bet he vacations in Hawaii with the wife and leaves the kids at home with a relative who owes him a huge favor.

The next morning, I filled the coolers with ice, packed up all the food, and then packed the suitcases, toys, and potties. As I fed the kids their breakfast, Scott once again did the amazing job of wedging everything back into the minivan.

We spent the rest of our first family vacation in our own house, swimming in our own pool.

We have since braved other family vacations that have been equally as bad, so to tell you the truth, I'm content to wait until the kids are in college. I'll send them a postcard when Scott and I go to Hawaii . . . alone.

Who Needs Rehab?

By Kae

Two months after Jessica took a giant tumble at gymnastics leaving in its wake two broken arms, we were gearing up for our summer in Florida. The days before we leave are always filled with packing, organizing our office files, and running what feels like thousands of work-related errands. This year, my "getting ready to leave for the summer stress" was increased the day Jessica finally got her casts off. The orthopedic surgeon it would take several months of rehab before she would be able to straighten her arms completely. I explained to the doctor that we were leaving for Florida for the summer and if she needed rehab he would have to send us home with the exercises or refer us to a rehab clinic in Florida.

True to her "I'm not a baby" mantra, in the two months she was in casts, Jess had managed to conquer feeding herself, dressing herself, and even using the bathroom without aid from an adult. Now that her casts were off, she was bound and determined to do everything for herself. The day before we left for Florida, I had to go to the copy shop to pick up some documents David had printed the night before. When we got there, Jessica unlatched her own seatbelt and opened the car door. She got out, closed the door, and turned to get onto the sidewalk. I stepped onto the sidewalk on the driver's side just in time to see Jessica stub her toe on the curb. She was going down and she couldn't put out her hands to catch herself. Everything seemed to happen in slow motion. I attempted to make a grab for her little body, but she was too far away. I watched helplessly while my child skidded across the concrete on the pointy parts of both elbows, scruffing up the delicate skin that hadn't seen the sun in eight weeks.

She hit the sidewalk and bounced once. I grabbed her; we rolled onto the sidewalk together, me on my backside, her in my lap.

"Oh, Jessica, you scared me half to death! Are you okay?" Tears were streaming down my face.

"I scared myself." Then she started to laugh. She had little tears on her checks, and I wiped them off with my fingers. She wiped mine off with her little tiny fingers.

During the previous eight weeks, I had berated myself endlessly because I hadn't been there when she was injured. I thought through all the scenarios of how I could have "saved" my child from the fall she'd taken. But I realized that day, sitting on the dirty sidewalk, that I couldn't even keep her from falling when she was five feet from me. So unless I could sprout wings and fly through a gymnasium, there was no way I could have protected her then. It was hard to accept. My being there or not being there would not have changed the outcome.

Our first few days in Florida were torture. Jessica is certainly not a baby, but she is stubborn as a mule. Once she decided she didn't like to do the exercises, each rehab session turned into as much a tug of wills as it was a tug at her frozen tendons. Frankly, neither seemed to want to budge. I had to find a better way to get these arms straightened out without causing any further psychological damage to mother or child.

Sitting by the edge of the pool watching the kids play, I watched as Christina climbed out of the pool. She used the side and the pushed herself up with her arms. Brilliant! It was the exact same move as the rehab exercises, but Jess would never know she was doing it—she would just think she was playing. I called her over to my lounge chair and told her from now on she was only allowed to get in and out of the pool from the sides. Under no circumstances was she allowed to use the stairs or the ladder. In the beginning, she struggled to get out and muttered constantly about how mean I was. Within a few days all the muttering and outright hostility she threw my way began to be worth it. She was definitely making progress in straightening her arms. By the end of the summer, she was climbing out of the pool without any effort at all. Not only were her elbows fully straightened, she had also rebuilt all the muscle strength that she'd lost.

When we came home, Jessica was able straighten her arms completely. She had a checkup and the orthopedist said she could go back to gymnastics. I thought about slipping the doctor a twenty to tell her that her gymnastics' days were over, but in the end I kept my twenty to pay for her new team leotard.

The first team practice back at the gymnastics center was terrifying for me. I sat with the other mothers, trying to keep up my end of the pleasant banter. Every time it was Christina's or Jessica's turn, I thought my heart would race right out of my body. By the time practice was over, I was drenched in sweat and emotionally exhausted. Jessica, meanwhile, prattled all the way home about what a wonderful time she'd had. I guess I was the only one of the two of us with post-traumatic stress syndrome.

Every practice got easier and easier for me. Each time the girls took a tumble, my heart leaped into my throat. Then I would see them get up, usually laughing, and give me a little wave. Big exhale; wait for the next tumble.

Jessica's arms healed completely. She still has one elbow that will hyperextend, but both her arms are the same length and the only physical scars are tiny little dots where the pin was where the skin doesn't tan.

I spent the next 13 years sitting in gymnastics centers all over middle Tennessee while my girls continued to see if they could give me a heart attack. Believe it or not, I eventually got used to it. There were a couple of hard falls, a broken wrist, and a broken hand. Yes, all were on Jessica. She's one tough cookie. Most kids would cry and carry on. She would just walk up to me, hold out an appendage, and ask, "Does this look right to you?"

Visiting Elmo

By Pam

I grew up loving animals. As a young child, our family always had dogs. I also had a love for rabbits. When I became a little older, I became a horse fanatic. My love for cats developed later in life and grew so strong that it turned into my profession: I became a cat behavior expert.

I also must preface this story by saying that I had no brothers, so my exposure to any creatures with antennae, scales, skin that sheds, or the capability of producing venom was nonexistent. As a result, I dreaded the day my son would discover the world of rodents and exotic pets. I have nothing against little mice, but I have spent a great deal of effort and money making sure they don't find their way into my house and, subsequently, into my cat's stomach with only a tail or other bloody body part left strewn across my kitchen floor.

Based on the glass-shattering screams that come out of my mouth when some unfortunate rodent finds its way into my house, there was little chance my impressions would change. I severely doubted there could be anything that would cause me to welcome one into my son's bedroom—let alone actually pay for the pleasure of having it under my roof and being responsible for its health and welfare. You can call it a cute little hamster, but it's still a rodent to me, and I pay a monthly fee to the local exterminator to keep those things from camping out in my kitchen.

One rainy day my kids were restless, so I decided it would be fun to take them to the pet supply store with me, since I had to buy some cat litter. I figured they could look at the fish and birds there. I guess in my previous visits to the pet supply store I hadn't paid attention to the section where the snakes, tarantulas, and scorpions were housed. So as Gracie and I were looking at the parakeets, Jack spotted a snake and pulled me over to see.

Even though he enjoyed looking at the snakes, it was one hairy little fellow sitting quietly in a terrarium that captured his heart . . . the tarantula. It had some long, impressive name, but to me he was just a big, hairy spider. I was extremely glad we were separated by thick glass.

"Can I have him, mommy?" Jack asked.

"No, honey, I'm sorry."

"Why?"

"Because we aren't prepared to take care of a tarantula," I responded.

"We can learn. We'll buy a book," he pleaded.

"You're too young to care for something that would require such special handling," I said. As soon as I said it, though, I realized this could mean he might ask for one again when he was older.

Gracie walked up to the terrarium and looked carefully at the tarantula. I was hoping she would shriek or recoil and not share Jack's desire to bring the little critter home. Instead, she said very matter-of-factly, "Mommy hates spiders, Jack."

"But he likes you, mommy," Jack said as he pointed to the tarantula who, ironically, had inched closer to where I was standing.

"Jack, you're three years old. You can't have a tarantula."

"But he's so cute and fuzzy," he said.

"Jack, we aren't going to get anything today except cat litter. Nothing that breathes, swims, crawls, slithers, hops, walks, or flies will be getting into our car. Now let's go."

Jack stood with his nose pressed against the tarantula's terrarium. The tarantula didn't seem the least bit afraid. It looked as if they were engaging in some secret communication. For all I knew, the tarantula was sizing Jack up as a potential lunch.

"You know, tarantulas are actually very nice," said a voice behind me. I spun around and saw one of the store associates—a man, of course. "For the right family, a tarantula makes a nice addition."

I glared at the store clerk. "We're not that family," I said, trying to insert as many icicles into my voice as possible, and took Jack and Gracie by the hands to find the cat litter.

After we paid for the cat litter and were heading out the door, Jack stopped in his tracks and started to cry.

"A tantrum will do you no good, mister," I warned. "We're not getting a tarantula."

"Can we visit him again someday?" he asked with tears streaming down his cheeks.

"If he's still here the next time we need food or litter, we'll stop and say hello," I assured him.

Elmo the tarantula (yes, Jack gave him a name) was a resident at the pet supply store for quite awhile. I guess the right family wasn't in a hurry to find him. So, lucky us, we were able to visit at least a dozen times. Jack conducted conversations with Elmo and interpreted what Elmo was saying to me (and about me, no doubt).

Amazingly, Elmo eventually found the right family, because one day when we visited, the clerk told us he had been sold. I don't even want to know what mother had okayed that decision. Jack was heartbroken, but I tried to assure him that Elmo was happy with his new family. With all due respect to tarantula enthusiasts out there, I was hoping that family wasn't one I knew.

I was grateful we no longer had to visit the tarantula, but for a while whenever Jack spotted a spider he was convinced it was one of Elmo's children, and he wouldn't let me kill it. For several weeks, I had to gently capture any spider that found its way into our home, and then carefully set it free in the backyard.

"Mom," asked Jack one day as we were driving by the pet supply store, "Can I get a scorpion?"

Easter Bunnies in Training

By Kae

David and I are both self-employed and have been working out of our home for over two decades. Working from home has significant advantages, such as being able to pick any 60 hours a week you want to work, being able to do laundry and tax returns at the same time, and being with your children and spouse 24/7. One of the major downsides is that you can get so involved in work and child rearing that you forget to keep up with the outside world.

I am an accountant. From January to April 15, my workload is all consuming. During this time, David does the dishes, washes the clothes, cleans the house, takes care of the grocery shopping and cooking, and most of all, takes care of our children.

Late one Saturday night David came in the office in a panic. "Tomorrow is Easter," he informed me. "We haven't done anything for the kids. I'm going to Walmart and we'll put their baskets together when I get home." He grabbed his keys and off he went to procure the necessary Easter basket items for the children. Thank goodness we live in an age when stores stay open 24 hours a day; otherwise, Easter would have been ruined.

He came back home an hour or so later loaded down with bags of all things Easter: little yellow marshmallow chicks, robin's egg blue bubble gum, SweeTarts in the shapes of ducks and chicks, little football-shaped foil-covered chocolates, Peppermint Patties, and jelly beans. He'd bought Matthew a variety of Matchbox cars and the girls would each get a stuffed fuzzy bunny rabbit. Of course, no Easter basket is complete without the five-inch solid chocolate bunny rabbit, so there were three of those.

We spent the next hour putting together three awesome baskets and filling brightly colored plastic Easter eggs with gum, chocolate, SweeTarts, and other goodies. Each child was assigned a specific egg color: Matt had blue; Christina, yellow; Jessica, pink. We also made up three golden eggs, each containing a five-dollar bill.

We have a large master bedroom suite on our second floor. Because we also had three dogs who slept downstairs where the kids' rooms were, we set up the Easter egg hunt in our bedroom. Based on the age of the child, their eggs were "hidden" so that they could enjoy finding them but not get overly frustrated.

By the time the last egg was hidden and the baskets were arranged in front of the fireplace, it was about 2 a.m. David and I crawled into bed exhausted but pleased that our kids would not be scarred for life because we had missed the holiday. We were good parents.

The next morning when the kids woke up, David brought them upstairs for the Easter egg hunt. I sat in bed and drank my coffee, laughing as the kids walked right past their own eggs, only to find their brother's or sister's. We played the "hotter-colder" game until all the eggs had been found. (At least we hoped they found them all. Then again, it would not be the first time we found a wayward Easter egg in October while retrieving a shoe from under the bed.)

With the Easter egg hunt finished and the baskets pilfered and perused, it was time for breakfast. In honor of the holiday, I made homemade pancakes shaped like bunny rabbits for the kids. (Actually, the pancakes were the same as the squirrel pancakes I am famous for, but I shortened the tails.) When breakfast was finished, it was time for me to get back to work. I was walking back through the kitchen when the telephone rang. I answered the phone and wished my father-in-law a happy Easter.

"Today's not Easter, it's next Sunday," he informed me. My face began to tingle because all the blood had rushed to my feet. All I could think to say was, "Dad, I'll get David for you. I'm going to put you on hold so don't hang up." We had a big problem. "David, your father is on the phone," I yelled down the hallway. "Oh, and by the way, today is not Easter. It's next Sunday."

When David got off the phone and the kids were happily playing in the other room, he and I put our heads together to figure out what to do. The kids would be going back to school and preschool the next day, excited to tell all their friends about what the Easter bunny had left them. We were about to be outed. Among other things, it would be obvious that we are not churchgoers. We live in the Bible Belt, so this could not be good. It would also be obvious that we are just plain stupid, and now our kids were going to be made fun of by their friends because their parents didn't have a clue how to read a calendar.

A plan had hatched in my mind. I went to the kitchen and used the office telephone line to call the house line. Our home phone rang a couple of times while I walked into the kitchen, then I picked it up and began to talk loudly. "Hello, yes this is Mrs. Allen," I said as I walked into the room where the kids were playing. "Oh, hello, Mr. Easter Bunny." I had the kids' undivided attention.

"Uh huh," I said as I put a serious look on my face. "Oh, I see. That's terrible. Yes, yes we did have baskets and eggs this morning," I said, looking at the kids to make sure they were listening. "Oh, my! I don't want them to get into any trouble. I'll talk to the kids and make sure they understand how serious this is. Thank you, Mr. Easter Bunny. Good-bye."

I put the phone down and looked seriously at the kids, who were all staring at me with rapt attention. "Oh my, that was the Easter Bunny," I said. Their eyes were wide with disbelief that the Easter Bunny had called our house. "Today is not Easter, it's next week." I continued.

"Yes it is too, Easter. We got our baskets," Christina insisted.

"No, Easter is next Sunday. The Easter Bunny called to tell me that the little Easter-Bunnies-in-Training came to our house last night to practice sneaking in and hiding the eggs and leaving the baskets without waking anyone up."

"The Easter Bunnies have to be trained?" Christina asked with a puzzled look on her face. Matthew rushed to my rescue. "Of course they do, Christina. You don't think they just know how to hop in and not wake people up, do you?"

"It doesn't matter," I said, not wanting the kids to get sidetracked. "The thing is that the Easter-Bunnies-in-Training weren't supposed to leave the eggs and the baskets. They got confused, and now they are in big trouble with the Easter Bunny," I said, keeping my serious face on.

"Oh, no. I don't want the baby bunnies to get in trouble," Christina, the soft-hearted one, said.

"We just won't tell anyone," Matt suggested. "Then no one will know but us, and the little bunnies won't get in trouble."

"Matthew, that's a wonderful idea," I said with true happiness. "If you guys promise not to tell anyone, I'll call and tell the Easter Bunny, and then the Easter-Bunnies-in-Training won't get in any trouble."

"We won't tell," all three kids chimed in at the same time.

I picked up the phone and punched the buttons the appropriate number of times for the kids to think I was making a long distance telephone call. I assured the Easter Bunny that my children wouldn't tell anyone and told him that the Easter-Bunnies-in-Training should not get into trouble.

Okay, I know I might have crossed the line of parent-child trust in leading the children to believe the Easter Bunny really was mad at the Easter-Bunnies-in-Training, just to save myself from looking like an idiot the next day in front of the teachers and the other parents at the preschool. But frankly, if we can tell our children that there is a Santa Claus, a Tooth Fairy, and an Easter Bunny, then I think that, under the circumstances, it was quite reasonable to tell the kids there were Easter-Bunnies-in-Training.

About the Two Loons

Pam Johnson-Bennett

Pam is the host of the Animal Planet UK series "Psycho Kitty." In addition to co-authoring Panic Early, Panic Often and Cookies for Dinner, she is the author of seven best-selling books on cat behavior. Having begun her career in 1982, she is considered a pioneer in the field of cat behavior consulting. Her book, Think Like a Cat, is referred to by experts as the cat bible. Pam is a former vice president of the International Association of Animal Behavior Consultants and founder of the IAABC cat division. She served on the American Humane Association's Advisory Board on Animal Behavior and Training and also the AHA Cat Health and Welfare Forum. In addition to her work on national television, she is a frequent featured speaker at animal welfare conferences around the country.

Pam lives in Tennessee with her husband, Scott, and two children, Gracie (13) and Jack (11). They share their home with a rescued cat named Pearl, a Sheltie rescue named Griffin, and three goldfish. Don't tell anyone, but Pam has been training one of the goldfish. She clearly has too much time on her hands!

Pam's website: www.catbehaviorassociates.com.

Kae Allen

Kae is an accountant who lives in Tennessee with her husband, David, and their female Goldendoodle, Fred. Kae has three children: Matthew (32), Christina (29) and Jessica (26). She has spent the last 26 years building her accounting practice, restoring an antebellum home, and raising her three amazing children. Kae and David enjoyed a brief time of "empty nest" syndrome before becoming full-time guardians to David's octogenarian parents. Kae still loves to bowl. She bowls twice a week, is the secretary of two leagues and the association manager for her local association. During the writing of this book, all three of the Allen children became engaged. In true Allen fashion, all three kids were married within 15 months of each other, Jessica, of course, taking the lead. While Kae enjoys her role as grand-human to her six grand-dogs—Windsor, Little Man, Fuji, Bailey, Gauge, and Keegan—she is elated to be called Grandma by her first human grandchild, Tanner (once again, Jessica in the lead), and is anxiously waiting for her daughter Christi to give birth (it's a girl!) in the fall of 2015. While not exactly having an empty next, Dave and Kae are fulfilling their dreams of travel to exotic locations, playing lots of golf, and spending as much time in Florida as their crazy life will allow.

Visit our website:
www.twoloonsandabook.com

Follow Pam and Kae on Facebook
www.facebook.com/twoloonsandabook

Follow Pam and Kae on Twitter
www.twitter.com/2loonsandabook

www.ingramcontent.com/pod-product-compliance
Lightning Source LLC
Chambersburg PA
CBHW020202090426
42734CB00008B/918

9781887043182